STAGES

On dying, working, and feeling

By Rachel Kauder Nalebuff

Published by Thick Press
www.thickpress.com

Fourth printing

ISBN 978-1-7320666-2-5

Book design: Omnivore, Inc.
Editing: Thick Press
Typeface: Freight Big Light and Post Grotesk
Proofreading: Nora Gallagher
Printing: Asia Pacific Offset

FSC www.fsc.org MIX Paper from responsible sources FSC® C136333

With:

ANONYMOUS
EDNA ADAMS
MELODY BROWN
GEORGE ELEY
JENNIFER FLOOD-SUKHDEO
SIMON HIRSCHHORN
JOHN JACKSON
AGNES JOHNSON
KAITLYN KELLY
KERESHA MORRISON
GLENDALEE OLIVERA
SHARON PRAIGROD
CHANNEL REID
DANIEL REINGOLD
MOJDEH RUTIGLIANO
NICHOLAS SMITH
JOY SOLOMON
ANNE WEISBROD
ROSA WILLIAMS

It feels right, every time I take the train to the nursing home, that the tracks follow a river. The Hudson is wide and sleepy. I can imagine looking at it while dying.
The tri-state River Lethe.

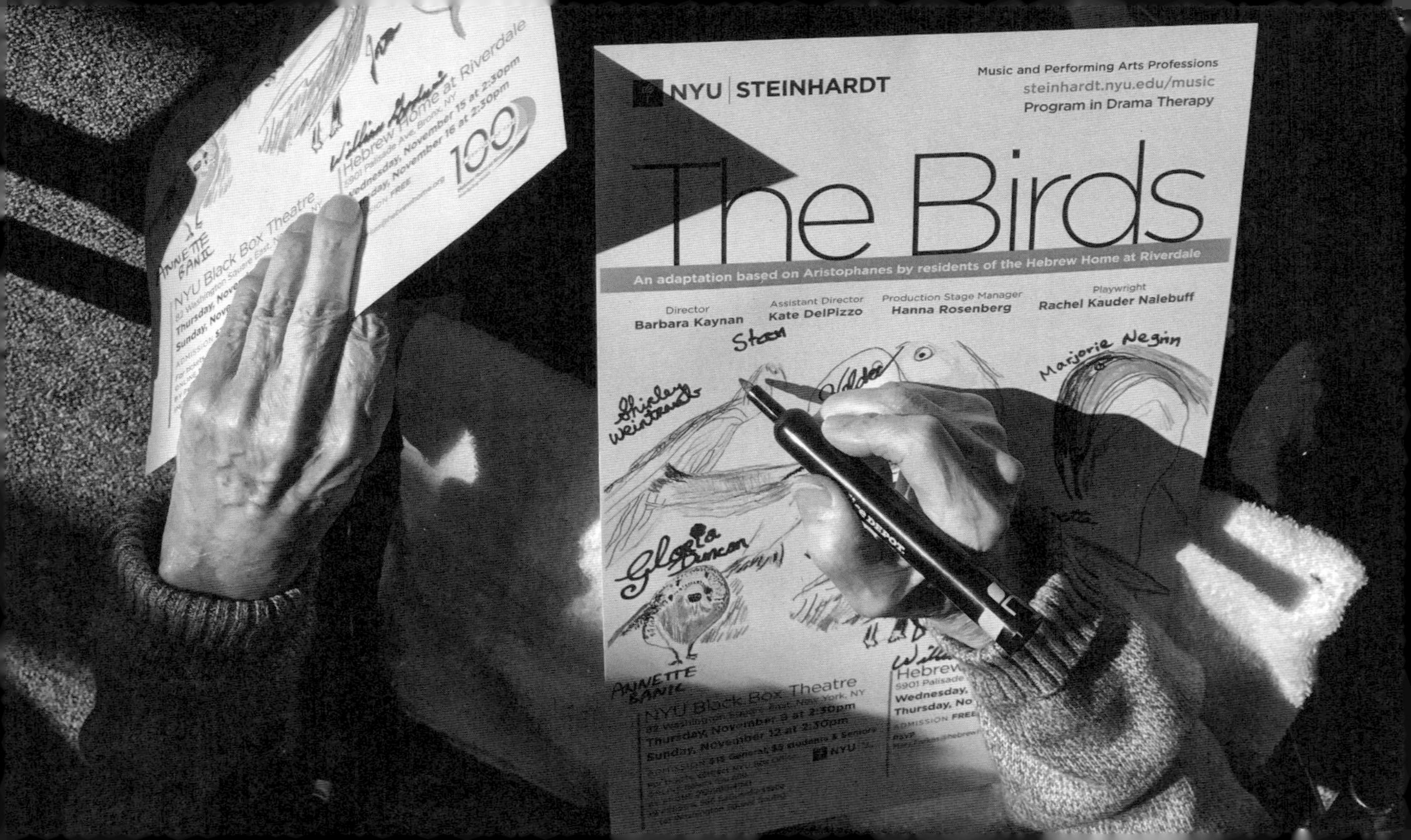

NYU | STEINHARDT
Music and Performing Arts Professions
steinhardt.nyu.edu/music
Program in Drama Therapy
The Birds
An adaptation based on Aristophanes by residents of the Hebrew Home at Riverdale
Director
Barbara Kaynan
Assistant Director
Kate DelPizzo
Production Stage Manager
Hanna Rosenberg
Playwright
Rachel Kauder Nalebuff
Marjorie Negrin
Shirley Weintraub
Gloria Duncan
ANNETTE BANIK
NYU Black Box Theatre
Thursday, November 9 at 2:30pm
Sunday, November 12 at 2:30pm
Hebrew Home at Riverdale
5901 Palisade Ave, Bronx, NY
Wednesday, November 15 at 2:30pm
Thursday, November 16 at 2:30pm
ADMISSION FREE

Residents sign show posters after their performance in our adaptation of *The Birds* by Aristophanes

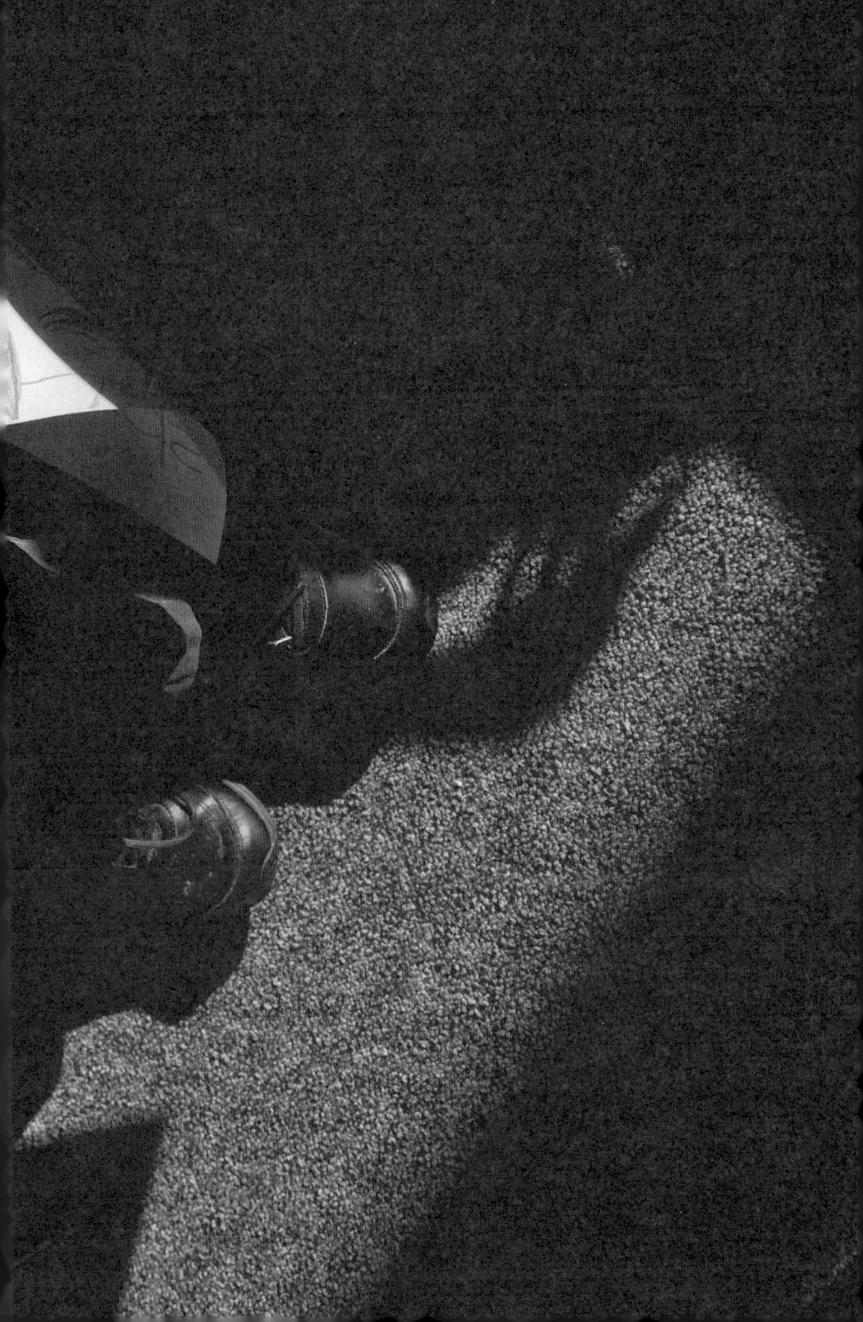

Two years ago, when I started working at the nursing home, residents used to scare me. Then my own friends started to scare me more. What were we doing with our twenty-something and thirty-something bodies! Why did no one acknowledge that whoever we love today will eventually die and that we'll find a new companion after! Why is everyone so concerned about the right career when professional adulthood is just one chapter of life!

I must fall in love tonight, I would think to myself on the train ride home. *To not let this phase of life pass me by*. And I would go home, and, at least for a few hours, really pay attention to the people and landscape around me.

On my first day working at the nursing home, everyone went around in a circle and explained why they had joined our community theater group. I said, *I'm interested in writing a play that expresses your stage of life. Both in the content and in the telling.* The woman next to me was asleep, so we skipped her. *I'm just here to kill the time,* said the next woman, flatly. She was wearing blackout sunglasses. This struck me as a much more honest answer for why we make art.

In the 1970s, Mierle Laderman Ukeles appointed herself as the artist-in-residence for the New York City Department of Sanitation. In her piece *Touch Sanitation Performance*, she shook the hands of thousands of sanitation workers and told them, "Thank you for keeping New York City alive!"

Technically, I have been hired by the art therapy department of a nursing home on a freelance basis. But I tell people that I'm "the writer-in-residence" of a nursing home. It makes me feel like I'm moving forward with my life. And I like the idea of a writer performing an essential function of a workplace without needing any explanation.

In the fall, when it came time to put on our play, I proposed adapting *The Birds*. The play follows the story of two Athenians who are forced to leave their home. Out of desperation, they settle in with a flock of birds. This doesn't go well. But with time, they come to understand that humans have much to learn from these tiny creatures who watch over everything.

Talking with residents about displacement and whether humans and birds can ever really live together and which kinds of birds they wanted to play and how they could listen to each other when half the group literally could not see or hear was the artwork.

A university brought the play to a small theater downtown. A lot of residents hadn't left the nursing home in years. Everyone was as excited about the show as the bus ride and eating shitty pizza that came from a real box.

Family members came. Students came for class credit. It was strange because people cried before the show started, just watching everyone in bird costume take their time getting on stage.

Now I am working on a play with staff. The nursing home wants me to study why some people have the fortitude to work alongside death and dying for decades, when most people burn out. Then I'm supposed to turn this information into an entertaining play.

But what I really want to do is make a ceremony. A ceremony for the staff of every nursing home across the country. Or no—a ceremony for everyone, across the country, who cares for the elderly, in facilities and in homes. Paid and unpaid. A ceremony where everyone would be honored for their service in keeping our elders ALIVE. And like veterans after serving in a war, everyone would be granted affordable health insurance, auto insurance and tuition rebates.

I think I might be working in the wrong medium.

ARTISTIC RELEASE FORM

I________________________ have reviewed the attached text and approve it to be included in *A Knock on the Door*. I hereby grant and authorize the Hebrew Home at Riverdale and Rachel Kauder Nalebuff to include this dialogue and excerpts of this dialogue in performances of *A Knock on the Door* and publication of the script. This authorization shall continue indefinitely, unless I otherwise revoke said authorization in writing.

__________________________ ______

[Name, printed] [Date]

____

[Signature]

If signed above, how would you like to be credited for your dialogue and participation in this artwork? We will list you however you prefer.
(Please circle one)

PERFORMANCES

1) Full name
2) First name only
3) Anonymous

PUBLISHED SCRIPT

1) Full name
2) First name only
3) Anonymous

In preparation for my interviews tomorrow, Maurice came over and we watched the link to Pawel's documentary *End of Life*. It was mostly close-up shots of people on their deathbeds. There's a lot of bleeding, crusty, flaky skin and people who take several minutes to swallow and get out one sentence. I felt bad that I had invited him over. *Isn't this romantic*, I said, laughing. Maurice thought about it and said, *Yes; if you actually think about it, yes.*

A conversation with Rosa Housekeeper 12 years

How did you become comfortable with death?

If you don't accomplish anything in life, you accomplish death.
I always wondered what life is like after death.
I've seen a lot of dead people. People who get shot.
How does it feel?
Where do people go?
I'm curious.
I've always been curious about how you take care of a wound.
How do you take a heart out?
I watched a lot of medical TV.
I wanted to be a mortician, but, I couldn't work while being in school.

Beyond your official position, what do you do here?

I'm a housekeeper, but I notice what people need.
I take people's shoes off. I turn the temperature up.
There's this woman who lives here who doesn't get a lot of visitors.
So I brought her a plant. This purple plant. Now she calls it her baby.
People ask me for favors—*Will you go buy donuts*? And I'll do it.
One woman gave me a shopping list for Walmart. And I did it! Sometimes because I feel bad. Sometimes because they're like family.

With your own money? On your own time?

Yes, on my own time!
The other day, I had to do something with my daughter, but I told her we had to stop at the dollar store because a resident wanted a hair scarf. My daughter's used to it. It's a part of her life.
I've bought residents wigs. Potato chips. Cheese puffs.
A lot of people lose socks in the laundry.

What is your advice about dying?

The "ShouldaWouldaCouldas." Don't let someone pass away with any of those.
Tomorrow isn't promised to anyone, so take care of those.
Reconcile with family.

How do you imagine death?

I imagine it just as being free.

A conversation with Nicholas Housekeeper 1.5 years

What is the word you prefer to use for dying?

Expire.

At first I thought I couldn't do this job.

Just to see someone sick. I would get sick.

In Jamaica, when someone dies they become *duppy* [Jamaican word for 'ghost'].

I grew up with people thinking that they see ghosts.

Whenever I go home, I always go back to people's graves and have conversations with people.

Now when I go back to Kingston, people say I bring all the duppies back into our home!

I don't try to think if this is real or not.

What changed so you could work here?

I just had to.

I'm still getting used to it. Seeing sickness and people dying.

Is there room to talk about this with other staff?

Yes.

What is the hardest part of this job?

Seeing residents unable to help themselves.

Knocking on a resident's door and a nurse saying to you that they've died.

What do you wish people outside the nursing home understood?

Once a man, twice a child.

When you get old, you go back to a baby stage. It's real. Caring for our loved ones. We should come see them even just to say hi or for a hug. It goes a long way for these residents.

So are you saying that emotional care is a part of your job? Did you think this would be a part of your job?

No. But working here brings you closer to love and caring.

Have you met this lady? [Pointing to a photograph on the wall behind me of a resident who appears blind]. She's a nice lady.

Who takes care of you?

[A long pause]

God.

During a break between interviews, I wandered down the hall looking for a water fountain but couldn't find one. I asked someone cleaning the carpet where to go and he said that all the water fountains had been taken away. Low-level contamination had been detected in the drinking water. All the water fountains had been removed from the walls so as not to jeopardize the residents' precarious health. I was holding out my water bottle, and he poured water from his own water bottle into mine. I insisted I would be able to make it through the day, but he insisted too.

A conversation with Agnes
Certified Nursing Assistant
26 years

What was your relationship to dying before you started working here?

As a young woman, I wasn't allowed to see people dying. So I had never seen it.
At first, here, I used to cry. When someone's condition was changing.
But as time goes on, it becomes a different thing.
Taking someone to the morgue.
When you wrap someone.

Sometimes, you see it. Right when their spirit comes out.
Then, your whole day. It becomes so sad. You can't even eat.
This is what it is? This is what's going to happen to me one day?

What does your job entail after someone dies?

Washing them. Turning them. Zipping them in the bag.
Everything has to be carefully done. You give them the best care.
Because it's finished.

What is the mindset you use to approach your work?

The floor is like a family to me. Even though it's always changing.
How was your night?
How was dinner?
You help with breakfast. You punch the elevator for people.
You live with them till God takes them.
My children never see old people here. In Africa, we grew up with them. We grow up with our grandparents.
Some of the residents cry to us:
I wish my daughter was here.
I wish I had a daughter.
I'm able to do this work because of where I come from.

What do you mean?

It's not about the money.
There is not enough money that could pay for this kind of work.
We are giving them the care that we give to our parents.

It goes both ways.
I've been a single mom since I was seven months pregnant. With my two kids. By the grace of God. My parents are in Africa. So many residents here have helped me raise my kids.

What do you wish would change about end-of-life care?

I wish there was more staff.

What is the hardest part of your job?

Challenging patients. I have one.
He is yelling all the time. He is young. But illness came young.

What do you do with challenging patients?

I remember that residents were like us before they came here.
I ask them to give me a chance.
I say: *If you give me a chance, we can help you have a peaceful month.*
Please give me a chance. Give me five minutes.
And you start from there.
They are human also. So your approach is everything.

I had coffee with a lawyer who had seen all of the world's darkness. I was telling her about interviewing nursing home staff and we started talking about how we harbor the delusion that we will 1) not die and 2) live to be old. At least in white, privileged circles, there is the sense that money can cure illness and buy longevity. So we are completely unprepared when death happens.

Two years ago, her little brother had died in an accident. She leaned over the table and whispered: *I tell all my friends, 'If you want your children to have a sibling to grow old with, you have to have at least three kids.' That's why we're getting pregnant this year. No one wants to hear it, but it's true.*

My grandmother hasn't been sleeping because my grandfather keeps waking her up to help him pee.

When I complain, she told me on the phone, *he says it's worse for him. But it's not that bad. Not sleeping.*

Now when I go out walking, I wonder how many seniors are inside the apartments around me. And how many people are also there, invisibly cleaning, wiping, carrying, listening, and tired of listening.

A conversation with Anne
Director of the Department of Social Services
31 years

What do you wish people outside the nursing home understood?

I'm struck by how few relatives know what their family members' wishes are.

There's much more than the DNR [Do Not Resuscitate] decision.
In general, do you want other people to make decisions for you?
Do you want to know what's wrong with you?
How often do you want family to visit you? When you're well and when you're not feeling well?
Who do you want to be around you?
What treatment do you want?
It's hard for family members to ask these questions, and unfortunately, rarely have end of life issues been discussed.

The decision-making process can be so much harder during a crisis when emotions are running high.

How could we talk about death better?

We have to help people know what questions to ask.
If families can open up and have these conversations before it's too late, it's a gift.
You don't have to have all these conversations in one shot.
Sometimes these conversations will go well, and other times they may not.

When should people start talking about these questions?

When I started this conversation with my parents, they said: *What, are you trying to kill us?!*
And I thought: *This is exactly why people don't want to have this conversation.*
You want to just say: *Of course not, of course not!* and end it there.

These conversations take time.

When Sam came over at night, the sky was bright pink like a conch shell.

We talked about how much pain is caused by thinking it's "too late."

I've never talked with my roommates about how we should all take out the trash, but now that we've lived together for a year, it's too late. I'll just continue taking out the trash myself, and resent everybody.

I've already been working alongside him for months. I can't ask him what his name is now! It's alright, I just won't know the name of the person who is eating their lunch while I am eating my lunch.

I've already invested ten years in the theater. It's too late. I'm stuck.

And we are in our twenties.

A conversation with Kaitlyn
End of Life Music Therapist
3 years

What is end of life music therapy?

It's about creating a beautiful supportive environment as people transition.

Sometimes it's about helping people regulate their breathing.

Matching their heart rate.

Playing the music they love.

Touching someone's hand, running my hand through someone's hair.

How did you get into this field?

I was a music therapy student and I had this experience in a hospital: I saw, truly, the most frail woman I have seen. And when I played music, this woman opened her eyes.

The light was now on.

What does a day at work look like?

I start my day at 8:30, 9:00, when most residents are still sleeping.

I check my email to see who died. Who made it. Who didn't.

Before I make rounds, I send out an in-memoriam email to everyone.

I could do better at the end of the day. I try to have some tea.

How do you make space for your own grief?

There's this metaphor from the play *Rabbit Hole* that grief is like having a rock in your pocket. Sometimes it's like a boulder. Some days it's jingling around. But it's always there even if, some days, you don't notice it.

When a resident that I connected with died, I used to find a rock on the grounds of the Hebrew Home and I'd take it with me. I kept these all in a vase in my house. But after 3 years, it was too much. 100 or so people died. But it felt like so much more. So I walked by the synagogue in my town and let them go.

It was a ritual that worked for a while. And then it stopped.

Walking is the best thing I can do.

What do you hope for the future of dying?

I want it to be as important as giving birth.

The same attention and the energy that goes into someone who is pregnant should go to someone dying.

Part of that is being really tender with that person. Lending them a hand.

Think about the "feeling state" around pregnancy: there's excitement, there's questions.

This is where we could do better for end of life.

People don't often ask: *How do you feel?*
How do you want to die?

What would you want your own death to look like?

I want to think of it as 9 months.
I'd want to talk about it with the people in my life, like a baby shower, where we all celebrate how great life was. To honor and thank people.

A conversation with Keresha
Cashier in the Cafeteria
12 years

What is your role at the nursing home?

When I started, I was working as a waitress. People advised me to not get attached. You can get emotionally drained.
But I can't do that.
I know how she likes her bread, how she likes her coffee, that she plays the piano.

I got in trouble because one resident wouldn't eat from anyone except me. Because I reminded her of her daughter. Anything she wanted, as long as it wasn't going to kill her, was my command. If she wanted to listen to jazz, we'd listen to jazz. Other people on the unit would complain: *Again with the jazz?* Yes! Again with the jazz!

There are many residents who get no visitors.
You're their visitor.

I have a master's in mechanical engineering. But this is in my bones. My mom worked in a nursing home. She'd take me with her. I remember singing happy birthday to people in wheelchairs.
My mother always said: *This is someone's mother, someone's daughter. This is someone.*

How has working at the nursing home affected how you view life outside of here?

My mother is disabled. She's bed-ridden and non-verbal. Working here provided me with a lot of insight.
One resident here had a stroke, exactly like my mom, on the same side.
I expressed to her: *I feel like my mom's not trying.*
And she said, *Do you really believe that?*

We watch all these strong women growing up. I'm such a logical person that I never looked at the emotional changes that come with strokes. I never looked at how it could emotionally hinder things. *To see you like this is hard.*
The resident reminded me of the other side: *If it's hard for you guys, what do you think it's like for us?*
It was easy to see how her daughter judged her. It made me realize I was doing the same.
It takes a lot to stand on the edge and be yourself. The wind is literally against your back. And to be yourself now? And not afraid?
I try to remind people that they are not what is going to kill them.

They are not diabetes, cancer, even their old age.

I'm struck by how you do much more than your job title. This work is philosophy.

You cannot have a job like this and think it's just a job.
From the maintenance worker to the housekeeper to the person delivering the bed sheets, you have to love it.....Maybe payroll you don't, or HR, because you're not interacting with residents as often.

You are not here just to put a hard-boiled egg and toast on someone's plate.
It's not about picking up a plate.
It's about *saying* something as you place it.
It's about reminding them that they have choices.
The loss of control is one of the biggest hurdles we come across.

What was something you've said? Can you share a story with me?

One morning, I saw Miss M. was rested, but no one else on the unit was.
I said: *Did you all go out last night? It's like everybody snuck out to party, but you slept on the car ride back!*
She laughed. They love being reminded of when they really did sneak out.

I asked Maurice what he was thinking and he said: *it's too corny to tell you*. I said: *tell me*. He said: *You have a deep heart. And I wonder what I did to deserve this.*

"What did I do to deserve this."

I played the sentence over and over in my head. Something was dissonant. Maybe because I had only heard that phrase used in the context of some great misfortune. Or maybe because it seemed inconceivable to use these words about me.

A conversation with Jennifer
Director of Clinical Nutrition
23 years

23 years is a long time.

There've been so many changes in nutrition, for the better. We're focusing now on educating families as much as patients. There's much more palliative care.

When I first started working here, placing a G-tube was much more common. But now families are opting towards making the residents as comfortable as possible.

Oh no, what is a G-tube?

A gastrostomy tube.

Before, the conversation was: *Do you want a feeding tube or not?* And now it's more: *This is what to expect. There will be a decline in appetite. It's actually not painful to be dehydrated.*

We talk about how we want to feed the ones we love. But it's actually incredibly uncomfortable to force-feed people. As hard as it is for us, it's natural for them [to stop eating and drinking]. According to the literature, it's actually often a euphoric feeling. But for many families, and even staff, this can be very scary. You don't know what to do when someone you love stops eating and drinking.

We're often in direct conflict with a family over feeding a resident.

It's hard because you're not sure the resident is being remembered.

What does it mean to express care without food?

Sometimes it's just about staying with a resident.

For residents who don't get visitors, I know dietitians who stay past hours, just holding someone's hand. So they aren't alone. Just being a presence.

A lot of it is about pain management and comfort. Is their mouth dry? We'll get them a mouth swab. Are they listening to music they like?

Are there other misunderstandings people have about death?

I wish people knew that there's often a sigh of relief.

That not every death is so, so sad. People outside don't feel that way.

I'm not denying the sad part of it. We may not be ready. But they are ready to let go.

Some deaths are welcomed.

What have the successful deaths looked like from a nutritional standpoint? Maybe success is the wrong word to use, but...

When someone's on a "downward" and you can do something meaningful.

When you can say: *Forget about your diabetes now. What do you want to eat? What do you love?*

What is a "downward"?

It's a progression downward in food or fluid consistency for comfort and safety.

You go from Whole

to Soft Whole (avoiding fresh fruits and salads)

to Chopped

to Purée (like a baby food or a pudding)

to Thin

to Nectar

to Honey-thick (like if you poured honey out)

and then, occasionally, to Pudding-thick.

Thin liquids go down more quickly. If it's thicker, it gives them more time to manage.

How do you track everyone's diet? How do you observe everybody?

Nutrition is a team approach.

We keep an eye on residents as they eat.

You might notice someone coughing a lot. With dementia, a lot of patients will spit food out. So then you have to decide, is it behavioral, or is it actually a clinical condition. A lot of the time, the CNAs [Certified Nursing Assistants] will come in and say: *I was feeding so-and-so and it took 5 minutes for her to swallow.* And then we'll determine if it's time for a downgrade.

What's the hardest part of the job?

Feeling a real sense of loss.

When you're wearing both hats.

When you're feeling it as a loved one and staff.

We haven't done them recently.... what are they called...we'll do a "Miriam's Well" sometimes. A rabbi will go up to a Neighborhood [a residential zone served by the same staff] and sing a song, and they invite the families. It opens it up for the staff to say what they wanted to say.

You have such a strong human relationship, you can't just fill the room with the next person the next day. You have to *process* it.

Here, we have the luxury of knowing it's important to express how we feel. Because we are in this industry.

A conversation with Melody
Licensed Practical Nurse
3 years

What is your role at the nursing home?

My job is patient care.
But the job goes deeper than that.
The fear of just being alone—we try to eliminate that by being there for them and their families.

How do you do that for family members?

We help them know they've done their best.
We talk about the sick patient's life. Who we see them to be.
They can see: *Yes that was my mom, that was my dad, that was exactly how he was.* That gives them the reassurance that beyond the boundary of a family, we were also there. I love my job. Am I talking too fast?

No it's good. Even now, you're being so sensitive!

We also have a grieving process for residents. We'll bring together all the residents who live together on the unit with the deceased and light a candle. Social workers and the unit manager attend. The nurses on the unit are so busy, we sometimes can't set aside time to celebrate.

What is the hardest part of your job?

When I don't have adequate time in serving.
I want to do this for you. But I have to be somewhere else.
Even when I delegate, I feel that if *I* had done it, it would have been better.
Because it's about relationships. So people will say: *Why weren't you here? It's not the same.*
Working with seniors is also challenging because today, they're up, tomorrow, they're down. And they'll never be the same.

How do you have the fortitude to do this everyday?

You need to learn to defuse things.
Sometimes a resident is upset. I'll walk in and say: *Hi, how are you!!*
It's not about ignoring what's happening. But trying to restart things.
I'm not perfect. I get frustrated. But I don't carry yesterday with me.

How do you do that? That seems quite superhuman.

Everyday, before I get home, I sit in the car.
For 15 minutes. For half an hour. To clear my head.

I have two kids. I want to greet them. Once I'm home, I am completely with my family.

How has working here changed your understanding of dying?

No one is ever prepared or ready for death. No one says, by the age of 60: *I'm ready*.

There are people here that you can't mention the word "death" to!

But working as a nurse has helped me see that death is something we should not be so scared of. If we had a good life, there will be people to help me to travel the path.

I've worked hard, I was a good wife. I've been there for family. So when my time comes, people will be there for me.

I love the idea that the best thing to do to prepare for dying is to hold the ones you love close.

I say to my daughter who's 10 and my son who's 13: *I love you*.

And a lot of the time, they'll say: *Mommy I can't say it back, I'm on the phone with my friends!*

And I'll say: *LIFE IS SO SHORT! TELL YOUR MOMMY THAT EVERYDAY!*

That's all we have! Tell someone you love them. ...Kids today feel like it's about them and their friends!

Where did you get your ideas about that kind of caring for others?

I'm a child of God.

The God in me comes out in everything I do.

The need to become a nurse was in me since I was about...12 years old.

It's not about the salary. It's that I've contributed.

I live for other people. It's what makes my job profound.

A conversation with Channel
Waitress
13 years

I started working here when I was 18.

What was it like growing up in a nursing home? How did that influence you?

More patience.

Outside here, when I see elderly people out there, I try to help. Even if they don't ask me.

There's one lady in my mom's building who is 103. I always offer help.

What do you do that other people maybe don't notice?

Sometimes a resident will need help buttering their toast.

Sometimes I help people feed.

Sometimes it's just talking.

What's the hardest part of your job?

When you really get to know them and they pass away.

Especially when they say: *I'll see you tomorrow,* and they're not here. That's the saddest part.

How do you cope?

I take it one day at a time—that's all I can do, especially with people who you see everyday and they become like family. I just take it one day at a time.

What would you want to change about the world outside the nursing home?

More respect for the elderly.

More patience.

I wish people outside could understand that some days, your body is aching, you're depressed.

I see so many people get impatient when someone takes a while to get on the bus. *She's elderly, give her her time!* When you get there, you'll want to take your time. I wish there was a little more courtesy.

My mom always says: *Once an adult, twice a child.*

Man, I feel like being an adult is the most messed up part of life. [Laughs]

What do you do when you get home?

I have four kids. A dog.

I'm always caring for something—sorry, I should say somebody.

It makes me feel good. Knowing that I'm helping someone.

This question sounds childish, but... Why do you think more people aren't caring?

Patience.

You have to have patience.

With kids. With adults. With animals. With your work.
There's always gonna be something that makes you frustrated.

I had a resident who was having a bad day. He threw everything on the floor.
I said: *What's going on?*
He stuck his tongue out. And I laughed and I stuck my tongue back at him!
And he started laughing. I said: *You okay? You want something to eat now?*
If you show them you're calm, they're calm.

My grandmother has cared for my grandfather his whole life, but only now that he's homebound does he express thanks for her. *How could I live without her!* he joked to me on the phone. *You never could*, I wanted to say.

This is someone who I was afraid of as a child. Who I barely spoke to growing up. And now he asks me questions about the day-to-day of teaching. He wants to know about my romantic life. He says things now like, *As long as you are happy*.

A few months ago, I might have seen all of this as a cause for even more sadness. *But we were just starting to get close.* Now I see: this life between us is the gift that death brings.

Mireya posted an image about calling our elected officials to express dissent around family separations. *The trauma that is inflicted on children now will affect them for their lives.*

The sentence got into me. Into my head, into my body. I found myself absent-mindedly remembering the words while walking, while swimming. I wonder why these words and not others got me to pick up the phone. Why I hadn't picked up the phone before and how the right combination of words can make people physically *move.*

A conversation with Edna
Certified Nursing Assistant
33 years

What is your role at the nursing home?

I've worked with patients with dementia since day 1. At the bottom of this work is patience.

Where do you get your patience?

Some of it is because of where I am from.

In Ghana, there is more respect and discipline. It's true, there is the beating of children. But when an elder person starts talking, you listen. There is a certain level of fear and respect we have for elders.

That mentality is in me.

You see someone crying in a corner here. You go over, say their name and ask: *You okay? You need to go to the bathroom?* Everything changes. It's like a baby. You have to think for them. Sometimes, something that should take 1 minute takes half an hour.

What do you remember about when you started working here?

I was surprised these places exist.

In Ghana, family is bigger. There are cousins, brothers and sisters, uncles and aunties, nieces and nephews. There is always someone to take care of the elderly. We keep old people in the house.

Sometimes people in America want to keep loved ones in their home, but they are not capable. Here in America, a family is husband, wife, children, and maybe grandparents. And everyone here has to work.

So it is good to have professionals because not everyone is capable.

I saw a woman here who is so young! I thought: *What is she doing here?*

But both her daughters work full time.

How do you start your day?

I come in at 7:00 am and do rounds.

I give my showers first.

You give at least two showers before breakfast. Sometimes, by the end, you are wet from head to toe.

I dance with residents. I sing with residents. Sometimes during activities like trivia, I will whisper the answer to them. And the staff will say: *Edna go away! This is cheating!*

[Laughs]

What is the hardest part of your job?

When we are short on staff. When people call in sick, you still have to get the same work done.

What do you tell new staff who are just starting?

Treat every resident like your mother and father.
One time I saw my own friend here.
[Long pause]
I barely recognized her.
She was wearing sweat pants, she was in a wheelchair.
It was so hard. Because I knew what she was like.
And now she is in a wheelchair.

I cried the whole day.
We take care of people here, but we don't know their whole history.

How have things changed for you since you've worked here?

I'm 62. When I turned 60, things changed a lot.
When a resident scratches you, it affects you.
That could be <u>me</u>.
It makes me more patient.
I see family differently, too.
They don't always appreciate the work we do. 10–15 years ago, this made me upset. But now, I see it's maybe their own guilt for bringing their loved ones to a nursing home.

No matter how well you do, people will complain.
I take the good with the bad.
Sometimes it's rewarding. Sometimes a family will hold your hand and say: *Thank you for taking care of my mother*. That makes you feel good.

We talk about teachers and how they affect people. But it seems true here, too, as a nurse. You touch a resident, it touches their family. It ripples out.

It's like a ball—when you throw it to a wall it bounces back to you.
When it is my time, I want someone to take good care of me.

A conversation with Glendalee
Social worker
5 years

What is your role at the nursing home?

I'm a social worker at the Weinberg Center [the elder abuse shelter at the Hebrew Home].

Our victims cannot go to regular victim shelters because they are not designed for people over 65. We serve as a virtual home for the seniors and we place them on different units, depending on their medical needs.

What should people understand about elder abuse?

That it's connected to other problems. How we don't have enough resources for mental health, for substance abuse, for domestic work. For example, if housing were easy to get, then elders wouldn't be such prey. If people weren't so burnt out, if there were more support for domestic work, elders wouldn't receive as much abuse.

What does a day look like for you at work?

It could mean going with someone with a police escort to their apartment. Another day it might mean getting someone all new clothing.

How did you get into this line of work?

I was raised by my great grandmother. We slept in the same bed. That's where it started.

What do you wish would change in the culture around aging and dying?

We need to see aging as a PRIVILEGE.

To be 100 is a privilege.

There are people who die at 25.

Unfortunately, we live in a world where youth is more valuable than aging.

The cosmetic industry keeps us wanting to look young, dying our hair.

It's a moneymaking machine. There are a lot of people feeding that machine, earning their living by it, who make sure it stays strong.

Even in the photos we take for our PR, residents look polished. But that's not real. There is such a spectrum of what aging really looks like. We need to start there.

No polishing.

How can culture change to embrace the reality of what aging looks like?

I make it a point to bring my daughter here. I want her to not be afraid.

Older adults love children.
This should be a place that every kid can come visit.

What's the hardest part of the job?
Balance and boundaries.
90% of perpetrators are families.
I am helping people at the most vulnerable time in their lives.
It can become more than professional. I become their family.
It's especially hard when we share a culture.
I was also raised to respect my elders. If you get passed a cookie YOU TAKE IT.
When a resident says I am like their granddaughter, if they say they love me, I might say: *I love you, too*, but I have to remind them: I am not their granddaughter.

How do you take care of yourself?
When I get to my car, my day has ended.
I recharge my brain and soul with podcasts. Oprah. My daughter is an instant reset button.

A conversation with Joy
Director of the Weinberg Center for Elder Justice
14 years

What is your role at the nursing home?

I run the Weinberg Center for Elder Justice. I care about how we care.

1 out of 4 women are victims of domestic violence. We have so many women who work here. How are we taking special care of those people?

How are we creating resilience for our workers, because people are watching people die all the time. If a staff member has been taking care of a resident for years and that resident has just died, and then that staff member has to go into the dining room and help someone eat dinner, that can be so depleting. How are we creating space for that person? How are we supporting grieving? How do we support staff self-care?

How did you get into this line of work?

I was a prosecutor for ten years. I prosecuted family violence cases, including elder abuse. Then I ran an elder abuse unit at a legal justice center.

Domestic violence abuse shelters are made for women and children. But there was no version of safe shelter for older people. So I created the shelter here with the help of our CEO. Fourteen years ago. We were the first one to create an elder abuse shelter.

How common is elder abuse?

Elder abuse affects 1 in 10 people over 60.

What has surprised you about working here?

How people look away from aging and ageism. How we are an anti-aging culture. It's crazy.

Other cultures are more focused on growing old. 30% of the US will be over the age of 60 in America in 2050.

Something is going to have to change.

How do we prepare for that demographic shift?

We need to have more conversations about dying. Part of that is about seeing dying as a process. An event that happens over time.

How do we do that?

We need to start having an aging timeline.

We talk now about what happens when we're 0–1 or 2–4. We know exactly what to expect. I am 54 years old. My life between now and 75 is going to be super different than between 75–80. 80–90.

It's crazy that that roadmap doesn't exist. When everyone goes through that.

If you're lucky!

Yes, if you're lucky.

We also have to pay attention to how scary it must be.

I talk about community all the time, but dying is a solo journey.

It doesn't mean you can't be supported. So how do we make that less scary? How do we make that...joyful?

How do you foster a feeling of joy at the end?

I'll ask people: *What do you want this to look like a year from now?*

What's around you?

Who is around you?

What have you let go of?

What is it like there?

It's like being on a sailboat. Of course there are outside elements that we can't predict, but every conscious decision you're making is in service of getting to that place. During end-of-life doula training we learned to ask:

If you have regret, how do you give it closure?

How can I let go?

How can I forgive myself?

Or maybe it's not about forgiving.

Maybe it's about knowing what we're holding on to.

How could we have more of these conversations?

I think we need to "befriend heartbreak."

The philosopher David Whyte writes about how heartbreak is part of the "inevitable consequence of being." Whether it's because of love, or because someone dies. But on the other side of grief is...an awareness of what we had.

So if we can feel the feeling of heartbreak, of grief, that's when we know that something was dear. Without that, we become detached. Unmoored. Lost.

It sounds crass, but I want to see it on the website: "We do dying well."

Why is that crass? It's a service.

Exactly! We help people die with dignity. We should be proud of the work we do to support people in their journey of dying.

How do you give space for this at the same time that you have to run a facility? How do you create support for staff and families when someone needs to literally be there to open the door?

That's the question.

The truth is, sometimes the staff will say: *It's better for me to go back to work*.

A couple years ago, I was very upset, because when residents died, their belongings were stored in a box in the basement

of the building until family members came to retrieve them. So we designed a space where families could come, pick up their loved one's belongings, write some memories in a journal, have some tea.

It didn't work for many logistical reasons, mostly because families weren't using the space, but we are still thinking about how to make the process sensitive to those in mourning.

I still think we need to have the support to sit quietly. Time to write about a resident. Everyone's coping mechanisms are different. Maybe people want to have some time to text their kids to say: "I love you." We need to give people space to acknowledge what they're going through. It's true; they can't get the rest of the day off from work. But we can create a self-care structure here for them.

When people talk about technology taking over, I think about this world of human services. And how what we really need are people.

A Conversation with George
Senior Manager of Therapeutic Arts and Enrichment Programs
20 years

What does coordinating an activity entail?

Let me give you an example. Nancy Pelosi visited a month ago in the morning. We had to have a decent number of residents to come and greet her. We're not transporting boxes of tissue paper—we're dealing with people, so we have to take our time. Often, people don't want to go places. You can't speed people up, you can't rush feeding anyone. To have 70–80 residents downstairs, it took coordinating with a whole crew of staff.

It's coordinating a whole army!

Yes. To do that, you have to get staff to buy into your vision. It's hard to tell staff who feel underpaid or underappreciated to ask them to do more. That's a hard part of this job.

I took residents on a field trip to buy bras and underwear. People wanted to walk down the aisles by themselves. During field trips, they'll say, *Don't hover over me!*

They don't want to feel like they are being treated like children.

My job is to make sure everyone comes back the way they left. But I can't be overprotective.

What is something you wish more people understood about nursing homes?

There is so much adversity we as the staff encounter everyday in our lives.

You're dealing with loss and stress at home. You're dealing with loss and stress at work.

So then when you're asking someone to be a caretaker, it's already a lot to ask.

More facilities—hospitals, nursing homes, restaurants—we need places to care for our staff. It could be physical, it could be spiritual. Something as simple as giving someone 15 minutes to have tea. All we can do is give people resources.

How have things changed over the years you've worked here?

No one who lives here now was here when I started. I've seen this place completely recycle itself.

What do you hope for nursing home staff in the future?

A culture where we express our gratitude. A real thank you from

a supervisor goes a long way. People don't want a party once a year. That's not thanking them for the work they did today.

What's a challenge you face working in this industry?

We're trained to deal with loss, but often family members have no idea how to handle it.

People's guilt or lack of knowledge makes it hard. People get hurt when a resident spits food in their face. We have to explain: *This isn't the person who took you to the ballgame. This is a shell of who they were.*

How does working here affect how you view aging in your own life?

Parents don't always do the right thing. But as long as they haven't physically or mentally abused you, you gotta be there for them.

I'm the caretaker for my mother. I want to visit so much that my mom pushes. me. away.

Me, on the other hand—If you want to visit, that's fine. If you don't, that's fine. I don't want to be a burden.

Coleman called me late at night to talk through music for the show. He had been thinking about the internet and the absence of ceremony around death. *We mourned Anthony Bourdain, but like for two days, all on our phones. A police or school shooting might not even get that much. A week later it feels like it never happened...*

As Coleman kept talking, I started looking out the window.

I started thinking about how I've separated the politics of the nursing home from my own life. After interviews, I always want to shake someone and say, *How can you put people through abysses of grief without providing emotional resources! We're not just talking about physical exploitation, we're talking about the exploitation of people's souls!!!*

But the nursing home is just a microcosm of my world.

How is grief valued in my life?
Is it?

Growing up, my family talked about grief in terms of how quickly you could get back to work.

In the academic part of the city where we lived, there were no vigils. I never saw candles on the street.

Now, I take in my friends' sorrows alongside the tragedies of the world every day. In spare moments on the subway, on the toilet, in bed. But I rarely remember what I read.

Information, it seems, is not a substitute for grief.
Of course. *Of course.*

I think I need someone, someone in my life, someone in my real life, someone with power in my life to say: *Please take a minute.* Or I need some kind of value system, some kind of culture, some kind of circle, some kind of march, some kind of protest, some kind of hand on my shoulder in my real life to say: *Take some time. Please take time. Take time with others. This is as important as drinking water. This is important. To ignore this kills some essential part of you.*

When the people I interview are forced to rush through relentless loss, they become numb, unable to care for the next resident.

I have passed by so many griefs.

I am afraid.
I am afraid for myself.
And I am afraid of not caring because I *do* care. I care so much about the world. I think I do. No I do. I really do care.
Or I want to actually care.
And I am really afraid for the world if there are others like me, too.

The nursing home PR department wants to put out a press release even though I am not done with interviews and have not started the script. I tried my best to explain my concept.

I said: *The show will acknowledge all the gestures of care that people do in nursing homes beyond their job description. This project will make this invisible work visible.*

The PR lady said: *Isn't that just kindness?*

For a second I felt like I had been caught.

Like, is this whole project just about people being nice?

And is that not interesting to anyone?

Am I a fraud?

Does kindness not sell?

Is kindness not news?

I replied: *It is about kindness. But it's about how kindness, at the end of life is much more than a gesture. A housekeeper will notice that someone is lonely and buy her a plant. That woman will find the will to wake up the next day. A nurse will joke about someone being withdrawn, and they'll find the will to eat. Someone will notice someone is missing a sock, buy them one, and that prevents a foot infection. Kindness at the end is about so much more than kindness. It's about survival.*

But I wish I could have just said: *Yes. It is about kindness.*

A conversation with Anonymous 7 years

What is your role at the nursing home?

I help make sure everything runs smoothly upon death and shortly thereafter.

What are some logistics you navigate?

How are we are contacting family members during the process?

Do we have a standard way of doing that?

After someone dies, who is updating everyone?

Who is telling the finance department so that they don't call a grieving family with a bill?

How are we navigating the timely removal of bodies?

What do you do when someone dies but they share a room?

What if a family wants to travel to see them but there's someone else in the room?

We have over 300 deaths per year, so there's a lot to manage and communicate.

You can get desensitized.

What's the greatest challenge you face in your job?

The mixing of the human and the business side of things.

We're losing money with an empty bed. So it's like...how quickly can we turn things over. Once someone dies, you have to fill a bed.

You have to find a good way to compartmentalize things. The mixture of business and death is...it's very hard.

What do you want for the future of end of life care?

The population is shifting to living longer and being sicker.

We need more palliative care. More long-term memory care. To give residents and families more of a meaningful experience.

What would need to change for assisted living facilities and nursing homes to make that possible?

The ability to hire more staff.

The whole way we are covered by the state, through Medicaid. Enhancing the hospice benefits available through Medicare.

Letting people even know that these services are available way sooner so people aren't lost in paperwork during crises.

The stress level is a huge part of what makes this work challenging.

How did you come to work here?

Before this I was working in finance as an investment banker. That wasn't the life for me.

My mom was a licensed home nurse administrator. I saw how small things could make a little

difference in peoples' days. My office is on a resident floor. Pushing a resident down the hall, which otherwise would have taken them 30 minutes, and listening to people: I love that that's a part of my job.

A conversation with John
Engineer
39 years

What is your role at the nursing home?

I'm an engineer. But I'm also half social worker, half nurse, half everything. If you can't get in a room, I'm the person you call.

What does it mean when someone "can't get in a room"?

People are used to their own ways. They're used to their own apartments. They are not used to interacting with other cultures. Now they have a room. They need help, but they don't want help.

We had a situation once where a resident would not leave her room [for an appointment]. So I went in there and started looking at the ceiling.
She said: *Who are you?*
I said: *I'm John, who are you?*
She said: *What are you looking at?*
I said: *The ceiling. I think it's gonna fall down!*
She said: *Get me out of here!*
You can't just say: *Do this, Do that*. Five people have tried that already.

What was it like working here at the beginning?

I used to give up quicker.

Residents have a different way of letting out frustration than we do in the outside world. It may look like anger, but it's not.

How do you start your day?

I start on the 7th floor and go down in a spiral working my way down to 1.
I ask everyone along the way if they need anything fixed. The sinks are leaking, a bed is broken, a light is blinking. As I'm doing my job, I'm messing with residents at the same time.
[Laughs]

When I miss one of my good mornings, that's the hardest thing. Often I'm the one breaking the news to the next person down the hall.

How do you hold that grief?

A lot of them are sick already. I can tell. So we are mourning together already. By the time they go, it's a kind of a relief.

What's changed over the 39 years of working here?

We're taking in more sick people.
And residents are taller. They keep calling me to make beds longer! I have to extend so many beds. I don't know what we're feeding people today.

What do you wish people outside the nursing home understood?

I'll tell you a story. We are trying to develop a new center [an extension of the elder care facility]. I went to this community meeting to discuss it. I wanted to be impartial. But it was hard. I knew people don't want the traffic. I knew this wasn't in their plans when they bought their two million dollar home. But I wanted to tell them: *Do you not think you're going to get old someday?*

How does your day end?

At 3:45. But my day doesn't stop when I leave. I'll see people in parking lots trying to help elderly people into their cars. I'll put out my badge to show them, *I'm not trying to rob you, I just work at a nursing home. I know how to help.*

In our field, the job is never done.

You *take* someone to be your wife. *Or you break up.*

Our language encourages us towards relations of possession, dominance and destruction!!

To officiate a marriage, I searched for alternatives that sounded somewhat like English.

Com unal vows written for the union of Emma and Paul

EMMA AND PAUL
[*EMMAAAAA AND PAUULLLLL!!!*]

May you take joy in each other
[*From that, may we create more joy*]

May you use your talents to heal the world
[*May we join you*]

May you love bravely
[*May we love bravely*]

May you be unafraid of change
[*May we grow together*]

May you meet heartache with loving courage
[*We will be your ground floor*]

May your marriage be like this place. Daily and sacred. A place where you are restored. Where you are most vulnerable, and most brave.

Emma and Paul, are you ready to share your personal vows ~~now~~?

PF's VOWS EZG's VOWS

Do you have the rings?

Emma—will you place this ring on Paul's finger Paul—will you place the ring on Emma's finger

Emma and Paul—do you take this marriage as a part of you, do you promise to live by the vows you've made today?

By the power vested in me, this community, and the state of California, we now pronounce you married. You ~~may now~~ kiss each other!!!! You may all toot your

The moment when everyone exuberantly shouted the couple's names I felt the earth shake.

Whatever I thought about theater and performance and rituals or whatever it is that I do, I was wrong. It is not a story. It is not information. It is not entertainment. It is a windstorm of feelings, all different, that we collectively feel.

When the road opened up to this view, I thought: *this would be a lovely place to die*. I didn't think this in a dark sense. Just the sentence as it literally means. The whole journey of death. That it would be lovely in this canyon in California. I wanted to share the sentiment with my friends hosting me, but couldn't figure out how to say it without sounding off some alarm.

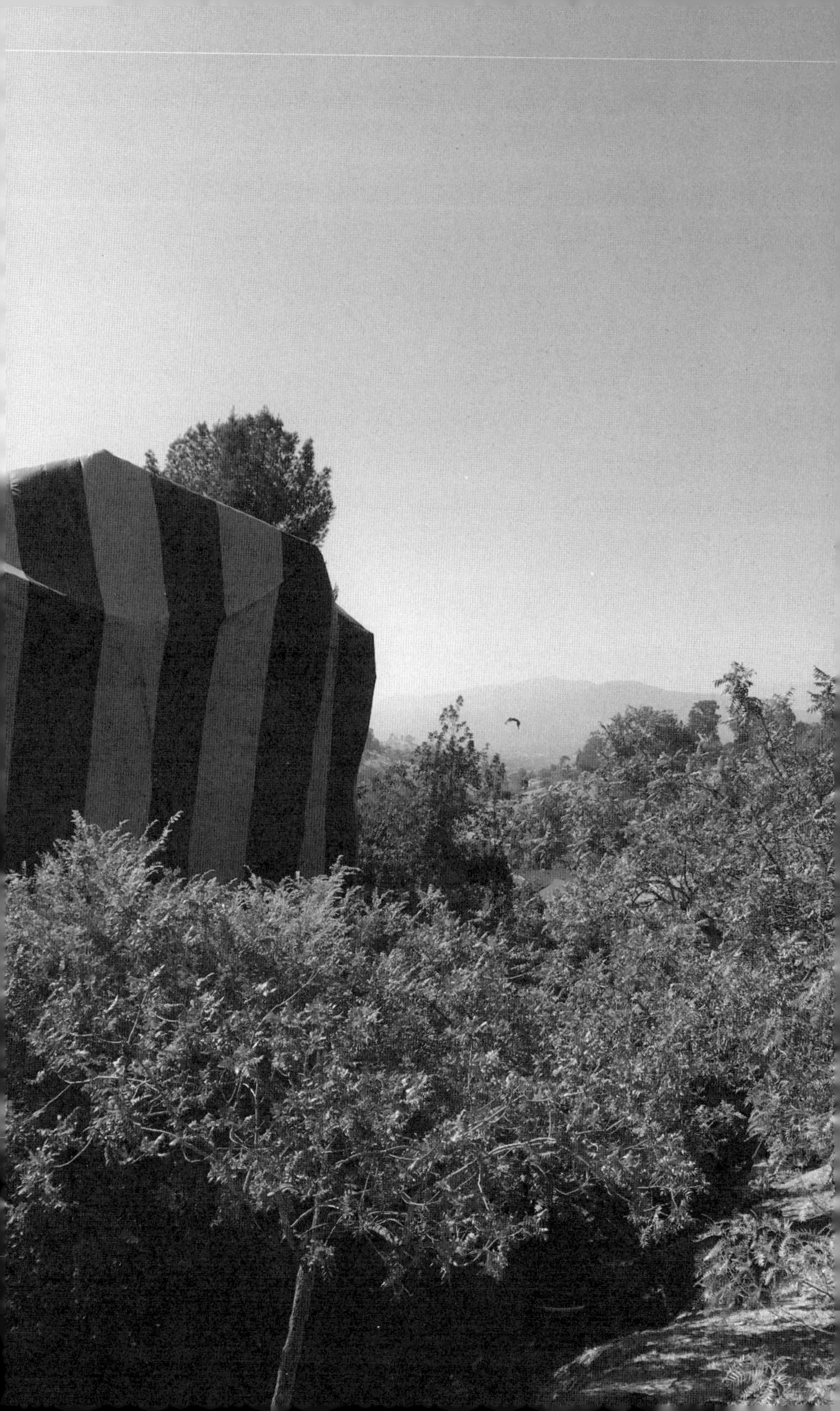

A conversation with Dan
CEO
28 years

How do you start your days?
With fires.

What are you working on right now?
I am helping start New York's first continuing care retirement community. I could spend all day thinking about any tiny design challenge for that project: What kind of doorknob should the rooms have so an arthritic hand can open a door? Or so people's hands don't get caught? People shrink as they get older, so how high should the doorknob be?

How has running a nursing home changed how you view aging and dying?
I want to stop you right there. It's aging and living.
When people say: *My grandmother died at the Hebrew Home*, I'll say: *No, your grandmother lived at the Hebrew Home.*

For most older adults, death is not their biggest concern.

What are people's biggest concerns?
Loss of independence.
Loss of loved ones.
Pain and suffering.
One resident said to me: *Death is my best friend. It's right at the door. I don't mind having it at the door.*

How does a nursing home help people with these other fears?
People don't have to face these fears in isolation.
What we do, really, is offer community. Community offers solace to grieve and to mourn.

What does providing that community look like, on a more institutional level, for grief and mourning? What could it look like?
We need to use the occasion of a resident's death as an occasion to celebrate a life.
When somebody dies, I imagine a time when everything on their Neighborhood [a residential zone served by the same staff] stops for a few moments of reflection. Perhaps the entire care team joins to transport the deceased together.

We had a resident who was 98. A nurse knew her so well, she came up to me and said: *She's on her way*. And she was right. So she was there at the very end. Just the fact that she had that kind of insight.

We need to be an industry where a nurse looks at her job as a sacred profession.

What would you like to see change in our culture around this chapter of life?

What families expect.
How we manage expectations.
People have extraordinary expectations of what we can do.
Families downplay the degree of their loved ones' frailty.

Why?

People are in denial.
There is a lesson we tell in the long-term care field: What is the difference between a nursing home and a hospice?

What's the difference?

When someone dies in hospice, people send a donation. But when someone dies in a nursing home, people might express anger.

What is behind our misguided expectations of nursing homes?

Whatever baggage that people are carrying is in FULL play by the time we see them.

Every family has "stuff." When mom or dad is at the end of life, it comes to the surface. Guilt over who is the caretaker. Who is sending the parent off. So now you're at a deathbed, and NOW you're going to talk about expectations?
[Shakes head]
It's easier to be angry at an institution than to face guilt or grief.

How could we better manage expectations?

I want to tell you what we've discovered. The length of a person's life does not necessarily get extended by medical intervention. People who pick the medical route are financially broken. And do not have quality time with their loved ones.
Just because we have this healthcare available doesn't mean we have to use it.

What about physician-assisted suicide?

It should absolutely be legal. If I had three months left, I'd say: *Let me spend time with family and then give me the pills.*

A conversation with Mojdeh
President of Nursing
13 years

What is your role at the nursing home?

I take care of the 600–700 nursing staff employees.

It's more administrative, but you can't take the nurse out of the girl. I was doing skin assessments over the weekend.

How did you get into this line of work?

I started out as a nurse in acute care where the goal is to fix people. When I worked in palliative and hospice care, I got to have time with people. On the floor, it's hard to have that time.

In this setting, most people are not coming here to get fixed.

What is the hardest part of working in this industry?

It's a lot to take care of people who are not in the "best of moods" on a daily basis.

Our family members have high expectations and staff often get yelled at. And by patients, too. Because, of course, people are unhappy.

People have lost everything.

What's changed since you started working here?

People don't need to leave their homes unless it's extreme. So people are coming in sicker.

A lot sicker. In 5–10 years, I think nursing homes will be mostly care for dementia and end of life.

How can we be prepared for this shift?

There needs to be a shift in how we view death. We need to talk more about the possibility that death can be beautiful.

How can death be beautiful?

One of my patients had terminal cancer. She was young. Her pain was a bear to manage. She was so bent on making it to Christmas. But she didn't think she could make it. So I talked to her kids and said, *While you're celebrating Thanksgiving... could you celebrate Christmas, too?* They celebrated the holidays at the same time. She passed the following week.

Are you saying that people could have more beautiful deaths by talking more explicitly about planning?

Yes.

How do we encourage a culture of talking about death this way?

The more exposed you are, the less shocked you are. I've pronounced a lot of people dead.

And for people who don't see death, it's about hearing them, too. Hearing their non-acceptance.

Hearing you talk, I wonder if everyone should be an apprentice to a hospice nurse.
Yes! Or a volunteer.

A conversation with Sharon
Palliative Care Manager & Clinical Nurse Manager
10 years

What do you do at the nursing home?

I'm here to make the process of leaving this world a little better.

None of us really know what's going to happen after death.

But the things leading up to it, we can take down some notches. So if I tell you, I can control the physical pain as much as possible—which is one of the biggest fears people have—that's one less thing off your plate.

If I can help you talk to the people you need to talk to, and say what you've needed to say, that's important.

I advocate for residents' best interest, which means always treating them with dignity and respect and honoring their wishes.

My job is to make the path as level as possible for your journey.

Can you talk about your work educating staff? People here keep referencing you when they share their philosophy on palliative care.

I am trying to make death and dying not a mystery.

A big part of what I do is teaching an approach to staff and residents that I have learned from all the patients, residents, families, and staff that came before them.

What gives you hope in this line of work?

That we may not live as a nuclear family anymore, but we can still act as one.

What do you wish people understood about dying, practically speaking?

It's important for everyone to talk about MOLST sooner.

What is a MOLST form?

That's a Medical Order Life-Sustaining Treatment form. *Do you want a DNR? Do you want a feeding tube? Do you want a trial of antibiotics and IVs?*

This is a conversation that should happen as soon as you get a car key. Parents should ask their kids. It should happen in both directions.

A lot of times families are making these important decisions for the residents, when they should be deciding themselves.

What do you wish people understood, holistically?

Death is a natural part of living; it is what all living things do.

I also wish people understood that most people don't die in physical pain. In a non-traumatic death, people stop feeling pain hours before they die.

But people can die in emotional pain and spiritual pain.

How could we better manage those kinds of pain?

Sometimes, it's as simple as holding someone's hand.

Sometimes, it's about peeling back layers to see what's preventing people from letting go.

Baggage is real.

Who is the person you need to talk to?

One patient, for example, wasn't letting go. I said to her family: *Has she talked to everybody?* Everyone said yes. They mentioned that she had a new great-grandchild.

I said: *Put her on the phone*. She heard her cry. And a few hours later, she passed.

Many times, our residents are just a shell of who they used to be. We tell their families:

The best part of them is in you already. You will never lose them.

She may not look like your mom, but what you have to do now is put your head on her chest and say I love you.

Zoe and I dug a hole in the ground. Tilly lay out in the sun as we were shoveling, and it felt like she knew what the hole was for.

I had never seen my dad really cry. When the vet told us we couldn't feed her anymore and that we just had to wait, my dad kept saying *this is so sad* in an unfamiliar high-pitched voice.

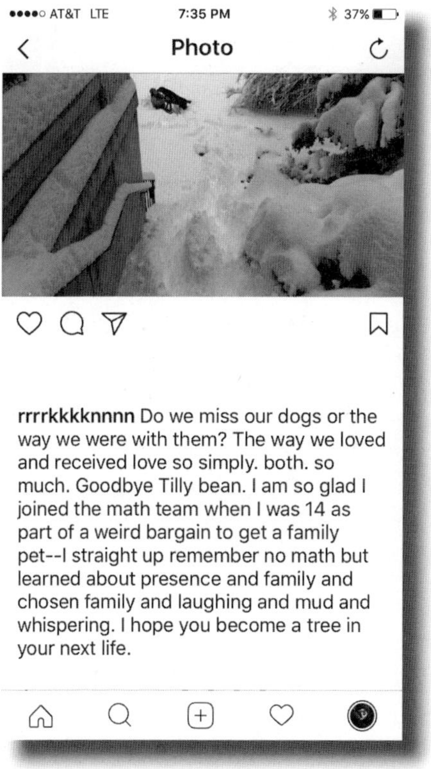

I have to work on my nursing home essay for the *Drama Therapy Review* and see Will's play but I just want to sit on the couch and be sad. I wish Maurice would know to be next to me while I am sad. I suppose I should tell him. Yes, I should tell him before I become even more sad because he hasn't proposed coming by. Maybe he thinks losing a dog is like losing a fish. Or maybe losing a fish is hard, I don't know. Grieving for an animal opens up something else.

I wonder what people think when they think of me

Do they think I am happy

Why don't I want to write plays anymore

Why don't I want to publish plays anymore

Why does my spirit shut down when I have to speak in front of anyone

It drains drains drains me.

I was leaving my apartment when dad called to tell me that Grandpa Edward was going to end his own life.

He had woken up and decided his life on dialysis wasn't worth living. And that was that.

When we got to Florida, Grandma Marcia was writing an email letting everyone know that Edward had only a few days left.

I need your help on this, she said to me. *You're an English major.*

In the mass email, Marcia wanted to explain that we weren't going to take any phone calls while Edward was dying. *He doesn't have the physical energy to speak to that many people. And I don't have it in me to talk about this.*

We wrote: "While we know you all would like to speak to Edward personally, thank you for refraining from calling us so that we can all be present together as a family during the week."

Should I include Bruce on here? Marcia yelled across the room. *And what about his fiancée?*

Sure, why not, Edward yelled back.

The next day, long emails from everyone in my grandfather's life started pouring in. Notes about how he'd been someone's mentor at the hospital, a beloved teacher, a friend.

We read each note out loud to Edward as he nodded and cried.

Soon after hearing all the letters, Edward died.

I held his hand and told him it was okay for him to go. Marcia kept screaming, asking if he was dead.

We told her that he was dying, that he was on the journey and she just kept saying, *But he could be sleeping!* I said: *Marcia now is the time to tell him it's okay, that we'll be okay, that he can let go.* But she held onto his shirt and said: *NO! I won't tell you that! Edward! Please! NO! Don't do this to me! I'm not ready! I'm not ready! Don't go! YOU ASSHOLE! I HAVE SO MUCH MORE TO TELL YOU.*

On the phone with her friends, Marcia kept saying: *You're going to have to teach me to live alone, how to put one foot in front of the other.*

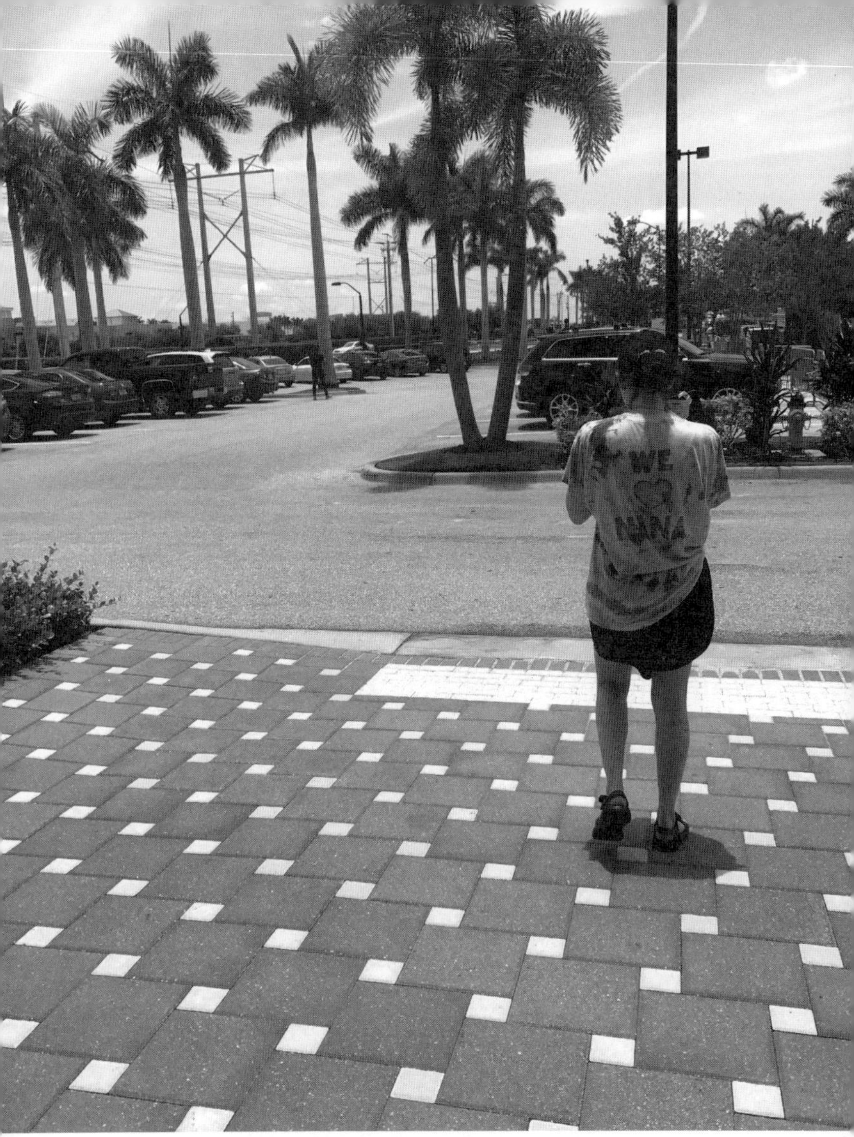

L.A. Fitness wouldn't let us terminate Edward's membership on the phone, so my sister and I drove there to deliver the message in person

I wanted to cry when we were sitting in the donut shop near my apartment.

How can you tell me so easily that you won't be there for the funeral? And then there is the wedding in Maine that I thought could be a romantic trip. *You don't have plans... but you're not sure you "want" to go?*

Instead I just nodded.

We were eating smoked fish in Marcia's living room when Martin, Edward's home aide, told me all about demons.

He said: *Whether you are a good person or a bad person, this doesn't matter so much. What matters is how attached you are to your demons.*

How do you detach from a demon? I asked. He had previously worked as an immigration enforcement officer so it was hard for me to stay completely open to what he was saying.

He said: *For example, I stared at my demon. The demon of promising, but not delivering. It was like a black horrible root in the earth. After three days of staring, the earth was scorched. It left a white scar. And it was gone.*

So now do you deliver on what you say?

Yes. He said, *But being late is still permissible.*

I laughed, but I saw from his face that he was not joking.

That is another demon, but not as big a demon.

Spending time with all the women in my family during *shiva* led me to have a vision. I imagined a pit filled with people—mostly women—running around, racing to catch people falling or holding other people up. Everyone is out of breath, in a state of panic, and almost no one benefits. This is what living in our society means. This is what being a woman in our society means.

What do I want?
I want to put everything away
I want to not travel for a long time
And I want to fall asleep next to you.

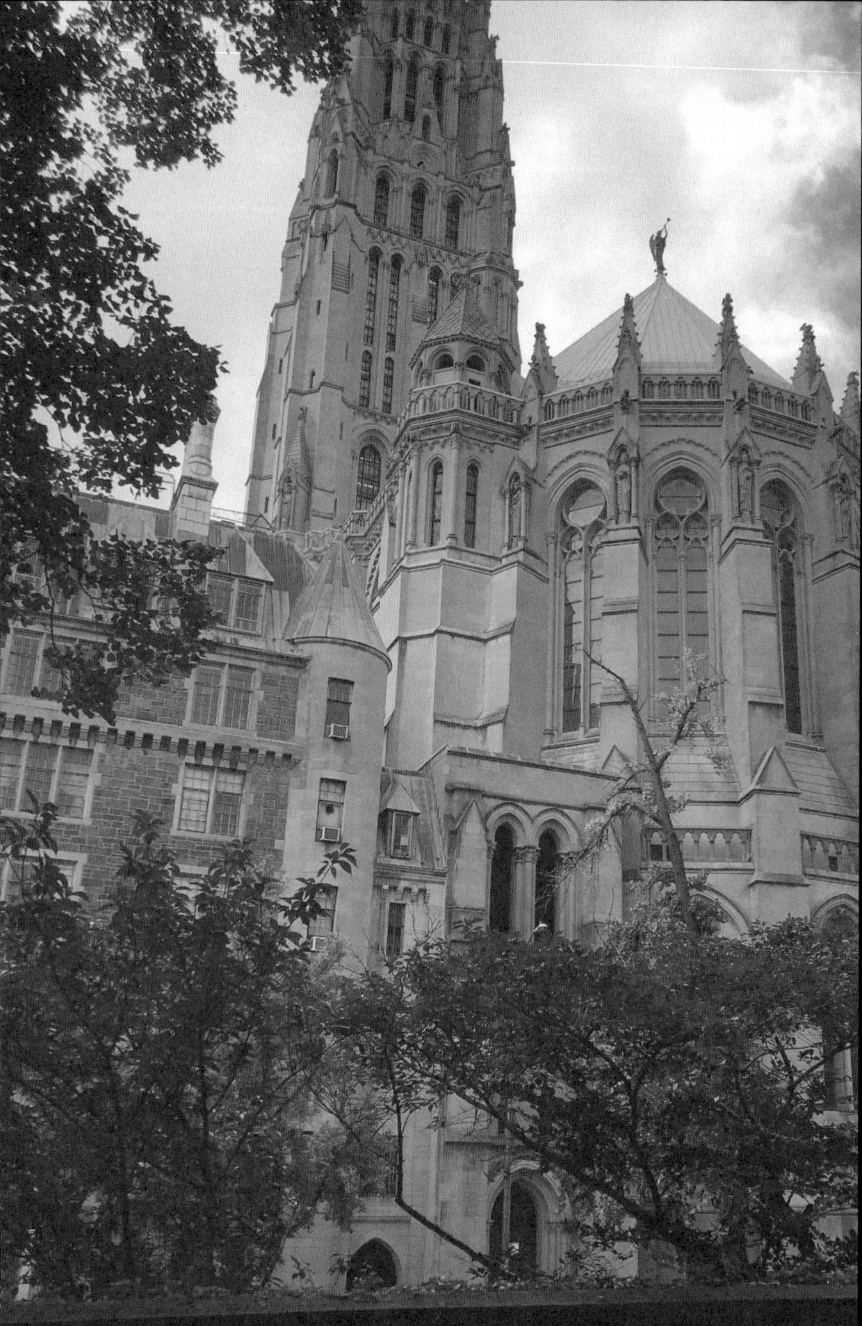

A site visit to the tower that will be our performance space

WHAT IS AMAZING ABOUT MAKING THEATER THROUGH A NURSING HOME

- I have never directed performers with this level of depth. They could say the word "banana" and it would make me cry.
- Everyone is getting paid.
- Rehearsal isn't cutting into anyone's break time.
- In these ways, working conditions are already better than in the theater.
- The art therapy department had to champion the idea of making a play. Then, several managers had to find and pay replacement staff to cover missing shifts. People outside the arts had to believe in this shit!

WHAT IS NOT GREAT

- It is unclear to me who wants and does not actually want to be in the show. Staff were "invited" to participate, but I'm not sure if people could ... say no? And then, for others, this is probably just a way to get out of work. Like a really weird, extended water break.
- Almost everyone has never performed and is incredibly nervous.

At rehearsal today, one person was running late because a resident needed help swallowing breakfast and someone else brought in their newborn baby and everyone was cooing and distracted and then we had only half the time left. But what can be done?

I couldn't be upset. The only answer is to change my expectations. If this is ultimately about staff resilience, life must unfold at its own pace during rehearsal.

But then, how can we be proud of what we make?

And how can the audience see it as beautiful?

Okay.

I have to help the audience redefine beauty.

Okay. This probably has to start with me.

How can I see this piece, with all its exposed seams, as beautiful?

Okay, okay, okay.

It won't be perfect. It won't be what I imagined.

Okay, at LEAST everyone has to be confident about where they are standing.

Okay. I have to cut all my ideas in half.

I have brought this upon myself.

The nursing home gave me 3 hours total with everyone to rehearse. They said this was a lot of time for them, and I said this was no time for me, but that I would try.

Why did I say this instead of saying: *If you want a beautiful show, you are going to need to give me time. But if you want something that does not make anyone tremble, I can do that in 3 hours, sure.*

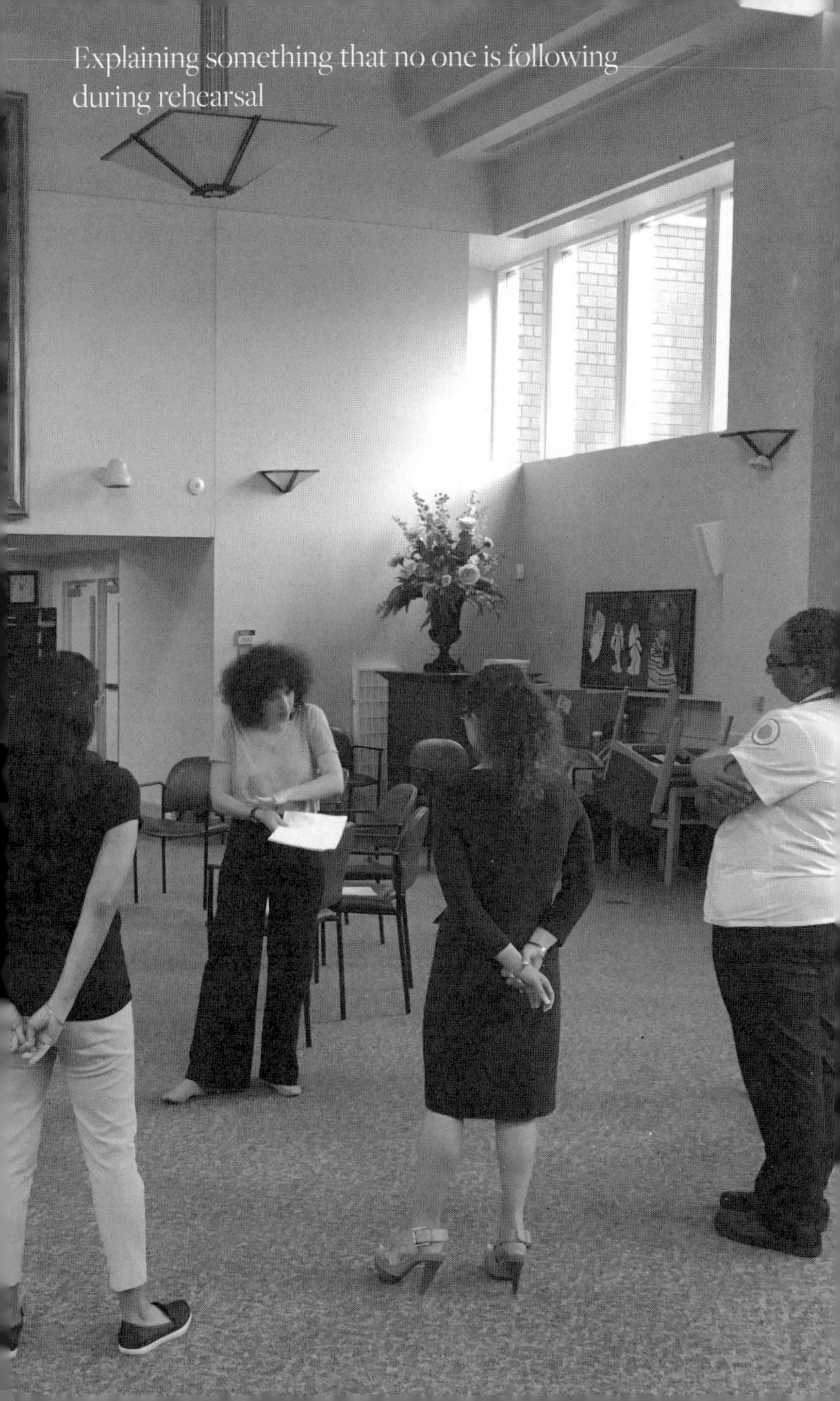

Explaining something that no one is following during rehearsal

I learned that my fall teaching job, which I thought was guaranteed, is not secure. I walked around New York City all afternoon dropping off books and visiting apartments with Zoe.

Then I bought a book and a pair of yellow shoes for an aspirational future in which I have a profession. I have so little time to read that these purchases feel equally delusional.

While walking, I remembered I'd had an epiphany. I couldn't remember what it was, but I remembered that I'd had one. I had been running. *I know what this show needs,* I remember thinking. *Bless this run!* I didn't write anything down because it felt like one of those realizations that changes your mindset, something you cannot forget.

But I did forget. I have no idea what the idea was. It feels like a discovery made in a dream that has slipped away. Because I wasn't disciplined enough to write it down. God, what is wrong with me.

I felt worthless all day. Like I have no skills and live wildly beyond my means. Hope tried to comfort me by leading me in an exercise where we write a CV but it lists our unmarketable and more spiritual skills.

On Hope's sheet she wrote: I can crack my ankles very loudly. I can feel genuine awe.

I wrote: eagerness to share art. Good at making noises while listening. Ease with the elderly. A love of patterns.

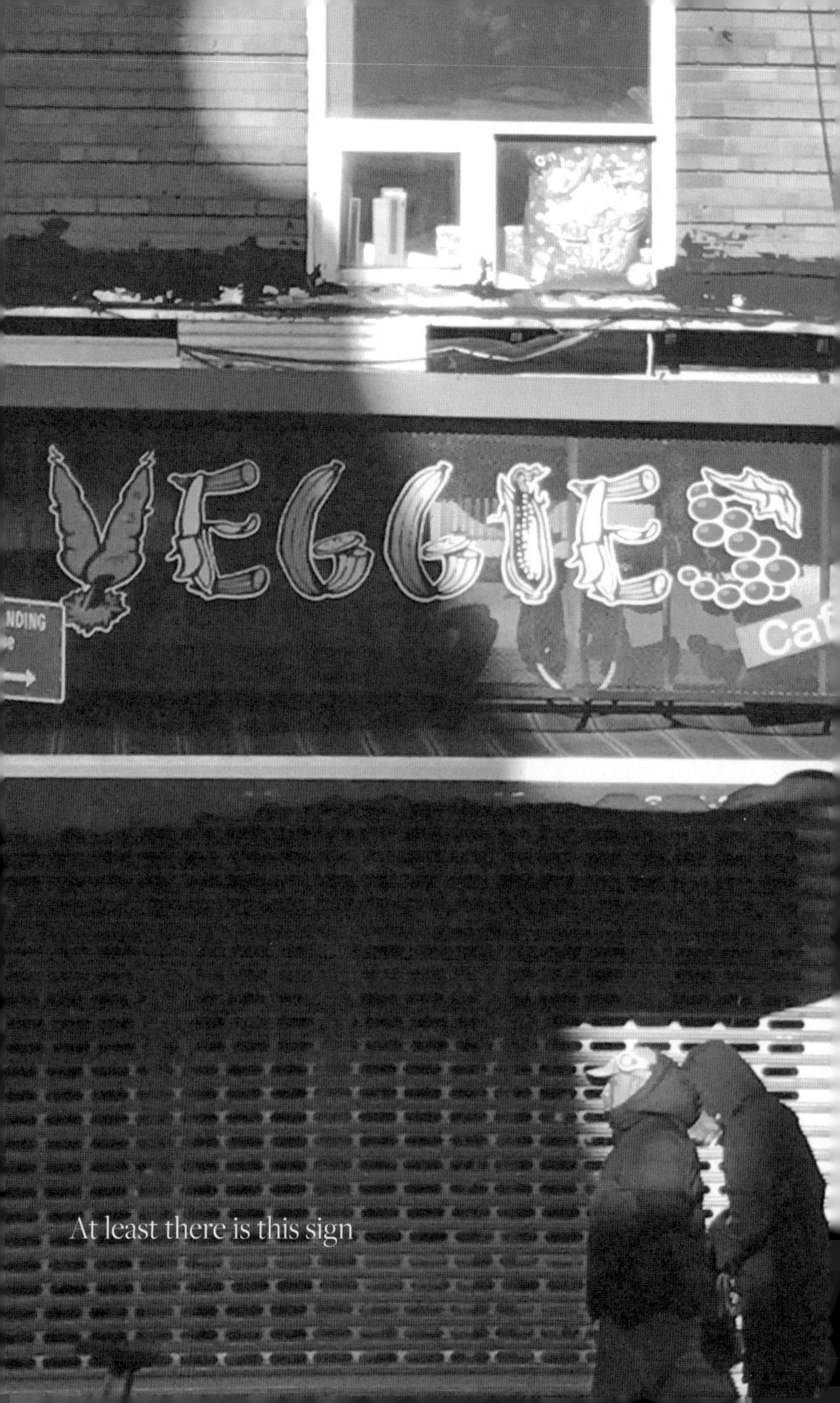

At least there is this sign

A British doctor created a rulebook for breaking bad news. I was listening to an interview with him on the radio. *Telling a patient how sick they are is one of the hardest parts of the job. So hard, that many doctors avoid sharing the full truth.*

He himself had been diagnosed with cancer. When an oncologist said to him, *I'm so sorry, this must feel terrible and frightening*, he burst into tears. He needed a doctor to recognize his emotional reality. It offered him a release, a permission to feel the heaviness he felt.

There is such a fear of negativity around me, and in me, too.

I remembered what the play needs to be.

It needs to offer time and space for grieving and memorializing and witnessing loss.

If the nursing home can't provide this time and space, can a performance?

Will an audience care? Will they feel it? Does it matter?

When I asked a performer if she'd like to take off her high heels for rehearsal, she looked at me and said, *Honey, if I can run a department in these, I can do this dance.*

She was not wrong.

As Coleman played piano and everyone got the hang of Rachel's choreography, there was laughter.

The group decided on their own that they wanted to start over from the top and get it right.

Coleman counted down 3 2 1. Again and again.

We only stopped when people started getting dizzy.

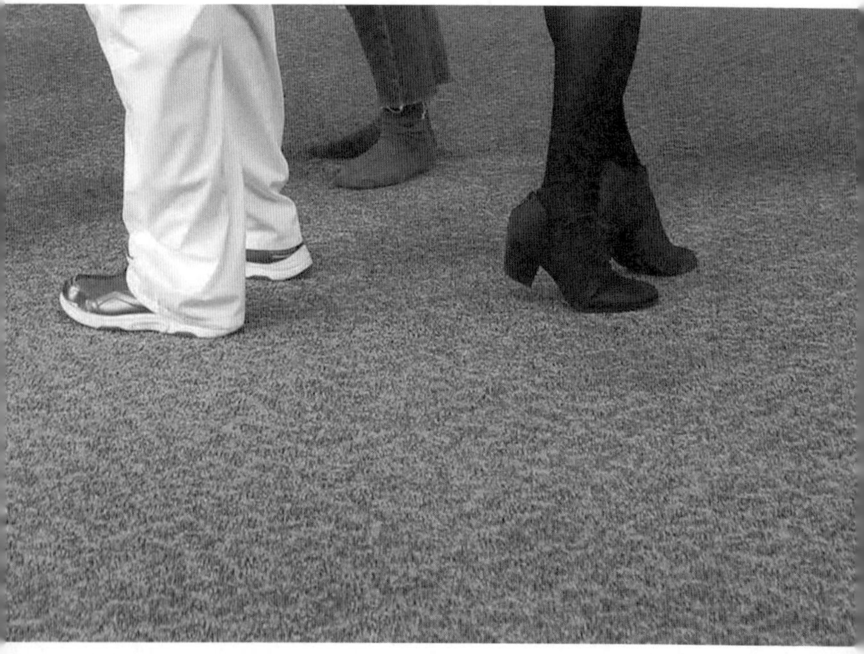

My grandmother told me a story on the phone.

Her neighbor's dog had died.

When she asked how he was doing, her neighbor reached out his hand across the lawn and started to cry. *My dog has been with me for seventeen years. I don't know how I'm going to sleep at night*! He was a large man, in his sixties. My grandmother somehow found herself cradling him in her arms.

I wanted to tell him, "Do you know who you're talking to?! I just lost my husband of 65 years! 17 years is nothing!"

I asked her if she had said anything and she said no. Because, ultimately, *grief is grief.*

Miranda bought us this mousetrap.

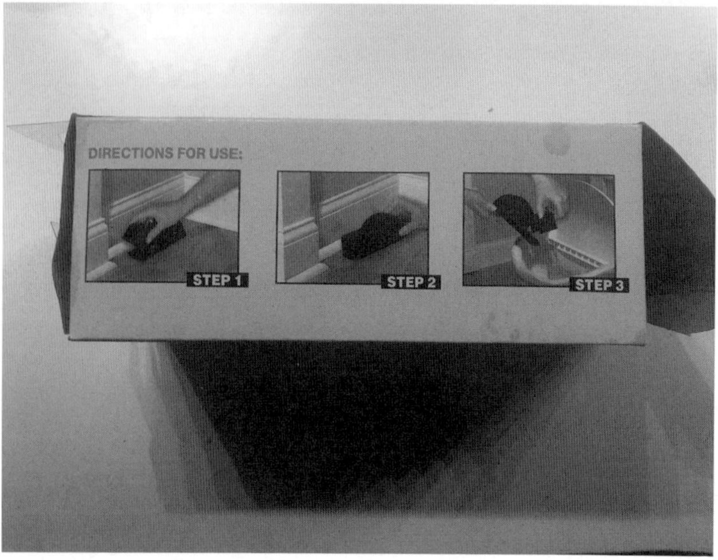

The packaging reads: *The unique design reduces the chance of accidentally coming into contact with a dead mouse.*

This says it all in terms of where we are with death. That we are so in denial of it, or having caused it, that encountering the mouse that we killed could be called "accidental."

While he was watching my play *Woe is Me*, Maurice was laughing deeply.

RACHEL, he said, afterwards. *I LOVED IT.*

I'm so glad.

No, really.

You seem worried? Were you worried you wouldn't?

No, I am just relieved that I loved it!

I was so relieved that he was relieved that I wasn't even hurt by his doubt. As he was reading my statement in the program, I could see his breath slowing down and him getting overwhelmed with a kind of love for me. I mean, writing is more honest to who I am than most conversation. So to see him love that and the play. I felt, truly, loved.

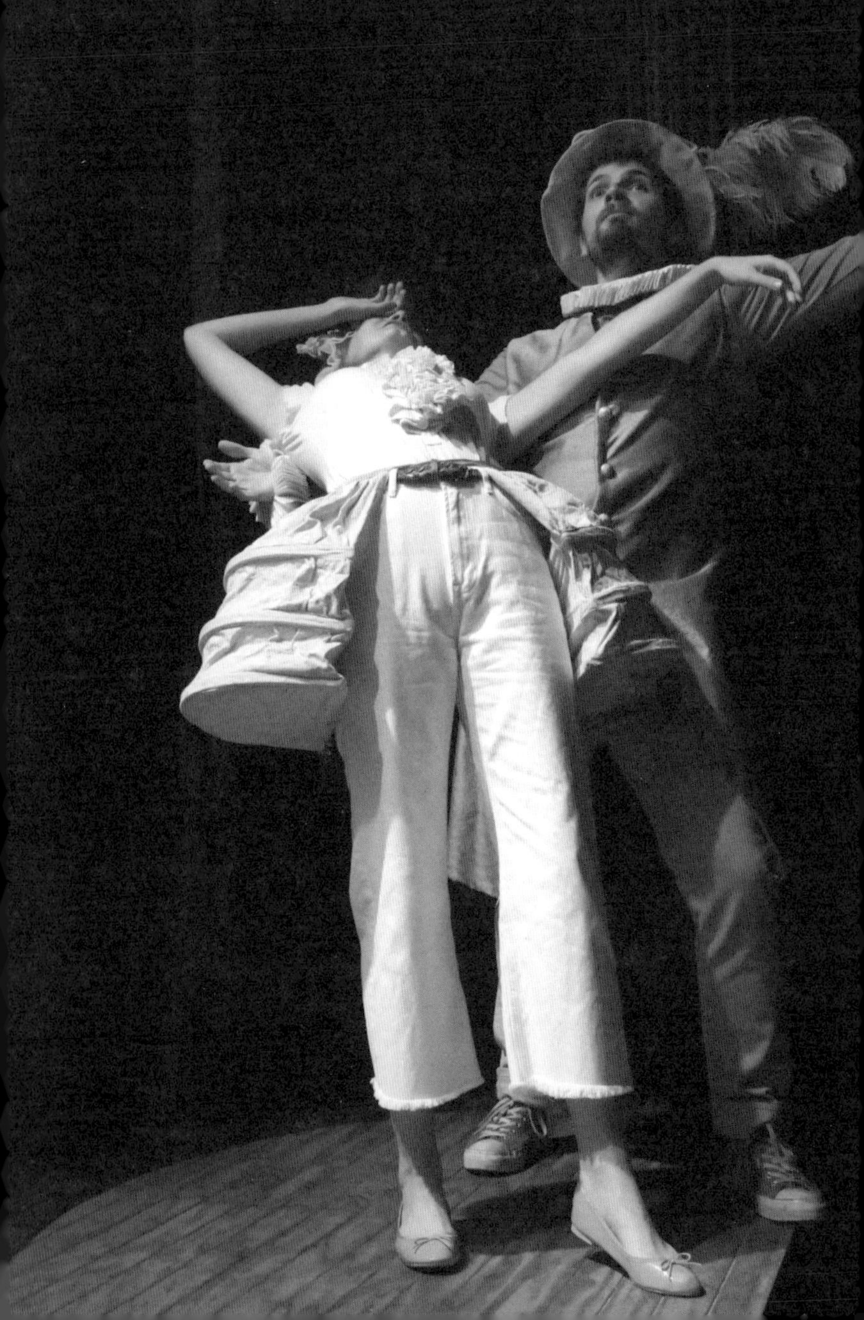

Rehearsal for my play about acting meant to be performed by acting students

A conversation with Simon
Director of Religious Affairs
23 years

What do you do at the nursing home?

The best way to describe my role is with this story: Many years ago, Itzhak Perlman had a concert in Carnegie Hall and was getting ready to go on stage. Once the maestro lifted the baton, in that moment of silence, there was a sound like a shotgun. People realized that a string of his violin had popped. But rather than getting ready to replace the broken string, he made a sign to the conductor to go on with the concert, which he played on 3 strings.

People were in awe and didn't stop applauding until he quieted them down by saying, *It is my genius to make music with what is left!*

My role at the Hebrew Home is exactly that: to help the residents to mourn what is broken in their lives. All the loss of people or loss of abilities. But also to also help them to make music with what is left.

Let's talk about mourning the broken string. I hear you were involved in starting a program for staff to mourn called Miriam's Well?

Do you know the story of Moses's sister Miriam?

Can you remind me?

Miriam played a very important role when the Jews were wandering for 40 years in the desert after leaving Egypt. Wherever the Jews were resting, there was always a well until she died. The well was linked with Miriam as a way to always give water and comfort to the people.

After September 11th I thought: *how can we share a moment like this together as a community of colleagues?* So I invited staff to a meeting I called "Around Miriam's Well."

I had thought about a physical representation of a well. We all came together in the Great Room and were sitting in concentric circles. We used this format at other tragic moments such as the big flood in the Philippines. This eventually developed into a program for staff and residents on the Neighborhoods [residential zones served by the same staff] for acknowledging when a fellow resident had died. It became a time to remember.

There are so few occasions to take a moment to remember that a person had died.

Is there a typical day for you here?

How do you define a pastoral visit? It's not like a doctor's visit. It's not visitation hours in my office. All day long, my encounters with residents, families and staff are a part of it. And they can happen at any place and at any time. At the cafeteria, during lunch, meeting with residents in their rooms or with families. These are very much pastoral moments. I also often get requests. For a moment of comfort, a personal crisis. Or to accompany a resident and often their family at the end of their life.

A special moment happens on Friday nights when I sing *Shalom Aleichem* and I make *Kiddush* [a blessing over wine or grape juice that sanctifies *Shabbat*] over the loudspeaker that is heard throughout the whole facility. It's a way to envelop the Hebrew Home with a prayer.

What does a pastoral visit entail?

I begin by making myself comfortable. Not because I like comfort. But because otherwise I will be standing thinking about my back. I make other people physically comfortable.

So we can be present.

[In a room where someone is dying], people will often speak to their loved ones and say: *Everything is going to be okay.* And then they go out of the room to start crying. And I'll say: *Those tears belong in the room. Those are expressions of love. They should be shared with the person.*

Even when people don't know what to say, I encourage them to just start a sentence....*It's hard for me to imagine a world without you*. That becomes an opening.

Can you tell me about one of your pastoral visits?

One day I got a call to come upstairs because a resident was dying. She did not have any family. The only ones there were the social worker and someone from therapeutic activities. They loved the resident. The two were huddling on the windowsill and I sat next to G.

They started to tell me about G.'s life, which had so many sad moments, but also how she was a fierce fighter. I learned that she had been married twice but never had children. They knew her story how she lost her first husband and then her second.

As they were talking about her, I was translating gently to her what I learned. At one point I said: *It must have been so sad to say goodbye to two men that you loved so dearly.*

G. had been essentially deaf, but I spoke very gently and I saw a tear rolling down her face. I was holding her hand. She moved her head on her pillow, just like a little child would do, trying to nestle into her mom's shoulder, and then she died.

What do you hope for the future of how we die?

We suffer, and this generation especially, we suffer from the Broken Toaster Syndrome.

What is the Broken Toaster Syndrome?

What do you do with a toaster when it's broken?

You throw it out?

There is a feeling that when we grow old we have become worthless.

I am not suggesting one should keep a broken toaster. They are cheap.

But life is not cheap. You cannot replace it.

Your beloved grandma who baked those marvelous cookies when you were young and gave you twenty dollars when you would go out with your girlfriend, when she got old and couldn't bake those cookies any longer and did not have access to her money, when she got older, did you stop loving her? Did she stop being your beloved grandma?

We are changing at every moment in life.

When this little boy turns into the young man or parents become empty nesters we have to redefine ourselves.

At every stage in life, we have to reimagine ourselves. And we need to do this with what is left.

We have to make music with what is left.

How do we reimagine dying? How do we become less afraid?

There is no app for that.

It has to do with being less afraid of our emotions.

When I visit with someone at the end of their life, I often test the waters by asking: *What do you think is happening?*

If they say: *Oh I got sick and I'll be better soon*, I know I don't have permission to go there.

But if they say: *Rabbi, I think this is my time*, I receive permission.

Not everyone is capable. A man really impressed me one day. He started the visit by asking me: *Rabbi, where am I going and what do I need to pack?*

What a courageous man. He wasn't even that old, but he knew he was dying.

It turned out that his task was not so much what he needed to pack, but rather what he needed to unpack.

Do you know the old Charlie Chaplin movies where he's going off into the sunset with a little backpack? If you ever asked yourself where he was going, he was going straight to the Hebrew Home.

When I can sit with a resident and
they allow me to look through
their little *pekalach* [Yiddish for
a small bag for sweets, or, more
colloquially, baggage], I feel
privileged.
I feel privileged when I can
accompany someone to the gate
at the end of their life they will
travel through.

Something about the rehearsal room was different today. More open and trusting. People had memorized their lines, and others had tucked folded scripts into their uniforms to refer to during the day.

When one performer delivered her monologue for the first time, she needed to take a moment to cry. But she wanted to keep going and everyone formed a circle around her.

The protective circle became a part of the show.

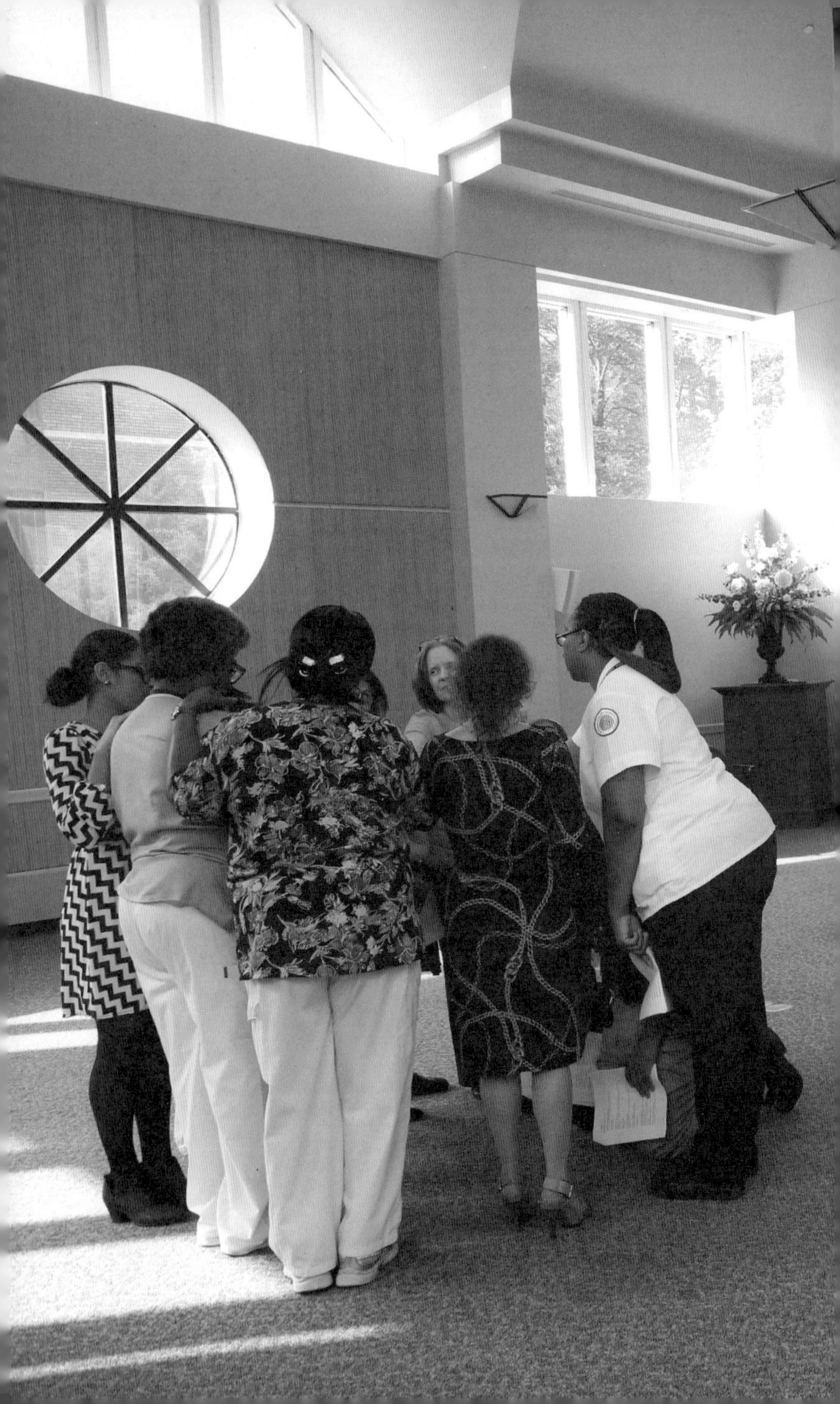

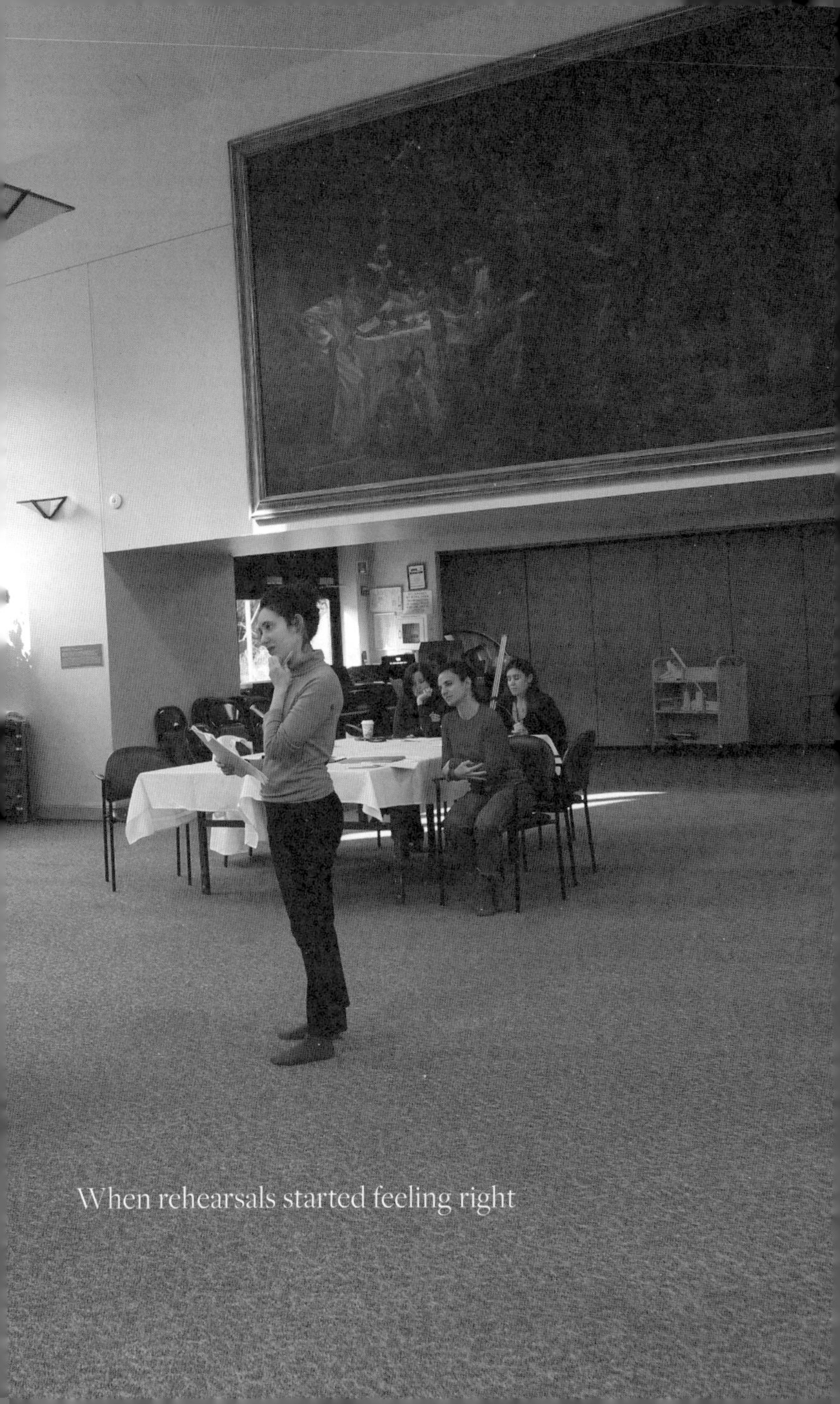

When rehearsals started feeling right

When Cassie and I went swimming in the Hamilton Fish pool and I came up for air between breast strokes and I saw all these New Yorkers around me and I knew Cassie was among them and so was my pool crush I felt so connected to everyone and the city, I felt a throbbing in my throat.

MSNBC was on and at full volume when I visited Grandma Marcia. She explained to me that she'd rather hear the sound of terrible news than silence.

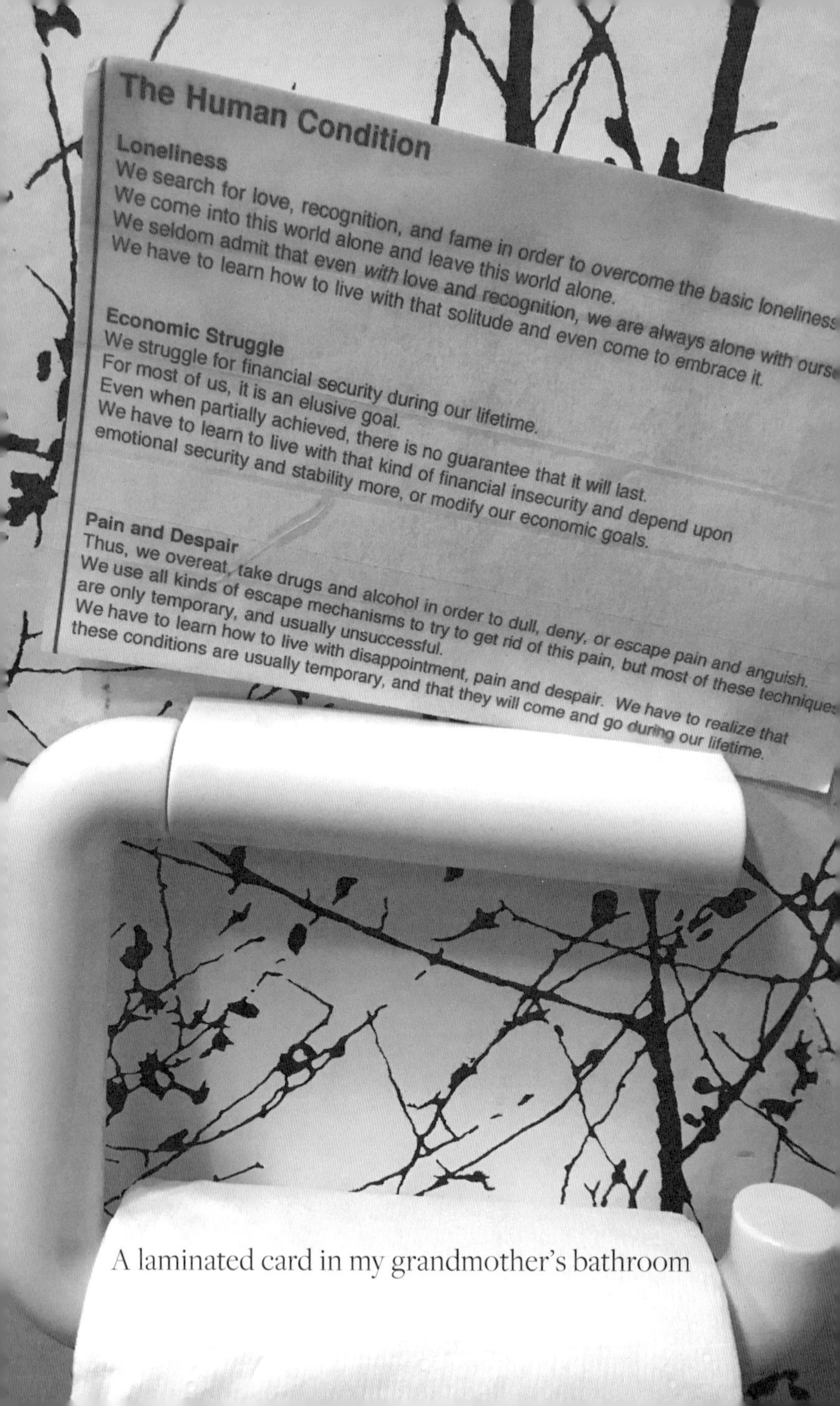

A laminated card in my grandmother's bathroom

I had a dream where my fears emerged, one by one, as if through a revolving door. I saw a vision of a barely alive mouse on the glue trap. I heard voices saying I couldn't teach, voices saying I'd never be capable of driving in the city, I heard Maurice saying he was in another relationship. This was all so painful, physically, like something had suddenly pinched my organs, that I woke up.

When I visited my parents, my mother took me to a community memorial service. It was in a dilapidated theater, and everyone in town was invited to share a memory on stage.

As a man was telling a story about sharing a bag of expired dried fruit with Joyce, which unbeknownst to them contained SPIDERS, I had a disembodied feeling. It was like I was attending my own funeral, I had a glimpse of how I'd be described.

Over her fifty-some-odd years, Joyce had collected hundreds of teacups with flower patterns. After sharing stories, everyone took a cup, filled it with Prosecco, and raised it to the spirit of our friend.

Whenever I feel sad around Maurice it is physical. I feel it in my hands. My throat. My vaginal canal. I wonder if this means that I am more in touch with myself or if I am being hurt more deeply than before.

Picture a bean with a shell.

I have been tapping on the outside of a heart, hoping something would change.

How did I let myself get into this situation?

It's over with Maurice. Or rather, it's onto the next phase. It took so long, so many drafts of thinking to arrive at the center: we love each other but this love doesn't translate to a relationship.

Is the end of a relationship its own kind of death?

In other words, is a relationship a life, something that we build together, and that we also need to grieve together?

Or, maybe, is this loss my own? And my sadness my own? Because I want to be loved, and loved without deliberation, and I am sad that this is not the case. Expressing my sadness feels like an expression of belief for what I deserve, what ought to be. The way Rabbi Hirschhorn talks about how sharing tears with someone who is dying is an expression of love for that person...in this instance, is crying an expression of self-love?

I invited Maurice over and asked if I could reflect on some of my favorite moments we'd shared as a couple. As I was reflecting, I started crying. Maurice wanted to share too. We kept thanking each other and crying and blowing our noses and trying to share more until our eyes were red and we were too exhausted to keep going. We brushed our teeth in silence. We fell asleep. I am sad and I am also at peace. Heavy and light.

The week of the show, I received an email from the nursing home saying they wanted to dedicate the play to the 19 people who were killed at the Tree of Life synagogue.

I felt like I needed to say, "Of course."

But what I believe is: *Here is the one night we have to give space to the people who work behind the scenes of loss. So to reorient our focus to the dead would be wrong. And....a dedication like this would reinforce the dynamic at the nursing home of privileging grief for Jewish lives over the needs of staff of color. So no. This show is not dedicated to people who were killed in Pittsburgh.*

I asked if the dedication could be made to those who will care for the victims' loved ones. But the idea had come from some higher up place in management, I was told, and there was no room for discussion.

I alternated between thinking: *This doesn't matter. It's a thirty second speech*, and then thinking: *NO, this matters. Because the pre-show speech is a tuning fork that prepares us for the value system of the show. And the value system of the show is a model for what could be the value system of our world. So the pre-show speech contains the seed to reimagine everything that is wrong or right about the world.*

During our dress rehearsal, the cast got nervous all over again.

What if I forget my lines? one person said.

You'll have your script in your hands, I said. *So you won't have to worry.*

But what if I forget how to read? They were totally serious.

I gave them my version of a pep talk: *All you have to do is be yourselves. That's what people are here to see and here to support. You. No one is expecting you to be actors. So if you are yourself, there are no mistakes.*

This calmed people down for a few minutes.

The show program

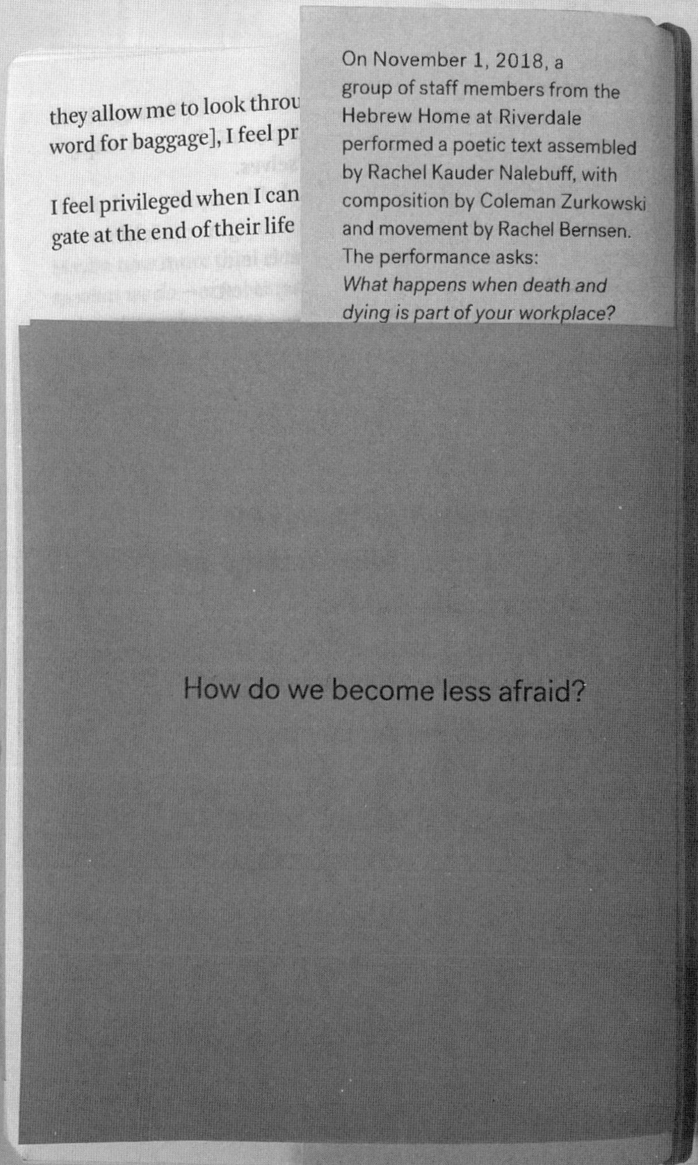

INTRODUCTION

This project is an exploration of resilience.

What is resilience? There are clinical definitions, but it's hard to distill what it looks like in action. But we can sense when it's present. And we know it's essential. So how do we build it? How do we care for our caregivers?

My colleagues and I discuss this idea regularly and, in conjunction with a myriad of other departments, began a deeper, more formal look at how resilience is created and sustained. To do so, we formed a caregiver resilience advisory council. We meet, as a group of caregivers across disciplines including administration, therapies, nursing, engineering, housekeeping and food services. Together, we ask and explore: how do we cultivate resilience in our community?

Death and dying comes up so much. Members said over and over again that this is the hardest part of their job.

As a drama therapist, I was excited by the idea of an arts-based inquiry into this exploration of resilience. There is something about sharing our words and telling our stories that makes sense. We all feel that and know that intuitively. When you speak your truth and are heard, you are in relationship. You are not existentially alone. Judith Herman, renowned trauma therapist, talks about how we are hurt in relationship and we heal in relationship. Theater is a fundamentally relational medium for exploration and communication. Whether it is between performers, audience members, or intra-relational, many levels of exploration occur in the dramatic process.

There is no "right or wrong" in creativity. Theatre is a beautiful, safe, and ritualized way to hold all perspectives.

So we decided to work in the framework of a play.

A major step in the journey was finding our way through the logistics. We had to weave an entire theatrical process into the busy day-to-day of jobs that matter a lot—the care of people. If a nurse leaves the floor for rehearsal, who steps in to make sure the care happens?

The Hebrew Home team demonstrated an intuitive understanding of why this process matters. The purpose of the piece as a tool (even an unconventional one!) to care for caregivers resonated deeply.

You could say this project started out of that commitment. How do we, as a society, show that caring for our caregivers is not extra? That it's essential to strengthening the fundamentally relational circle of care. And that without doing it, we won't have caregivers who will last. In listening, exploring, and sharing through this theatrical experience, we hope that we move closer to this goal.

The following conversations with our caregiving staff were conducted initially as both a way to support caregivers and to generate meaningful text for our play. Apart from sharing them in the form of production, the dialogues contain poetry and wisdom that applies to everyone who faces aging, illness, and loss. By encountering our

Introduction by Mary Farkas, former Director of Therapeutic Arts and Enrichment Program at the Hebrew Home

The show started with a moment of silence for the victims of the Pittsburgh shooting. The motions of taking silence seemed so familiar to the staff. No one seemed particularly moved or upset. I bet no one in the cathedral was upset except for me.

My "special events" silk shirt had ripped during rehearsal right in the armpit hole, so I didn't want to move my arms. Especially because I had recently stopped shaving my armpit hair. But all the performers were so nervous about where they needed to stand that they needed me on stage. So I conducted them with a giant hole in my right armpit and they were luminous.

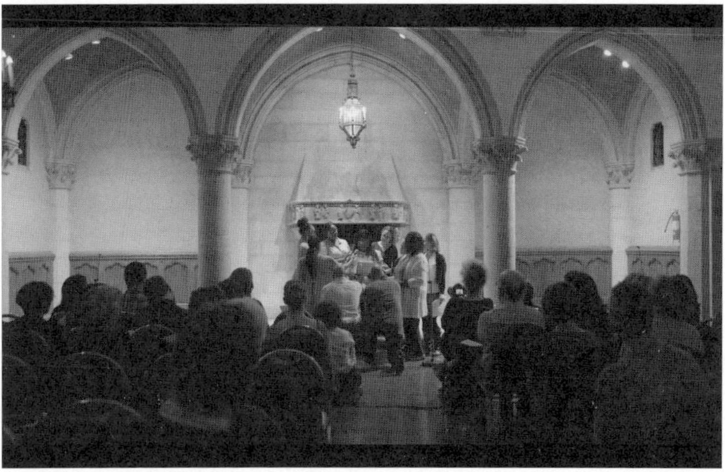

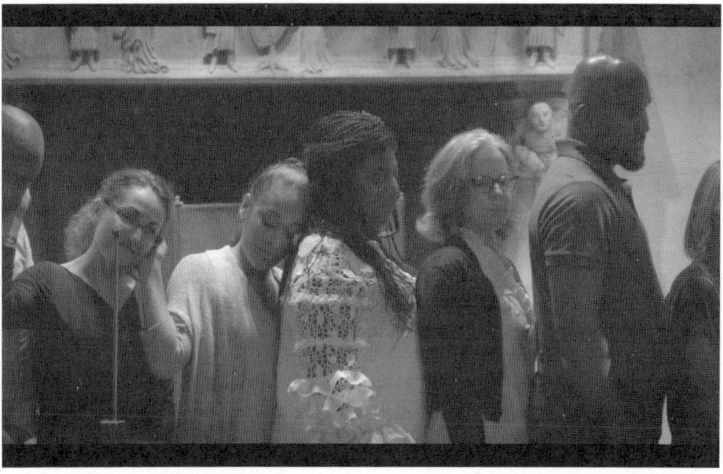

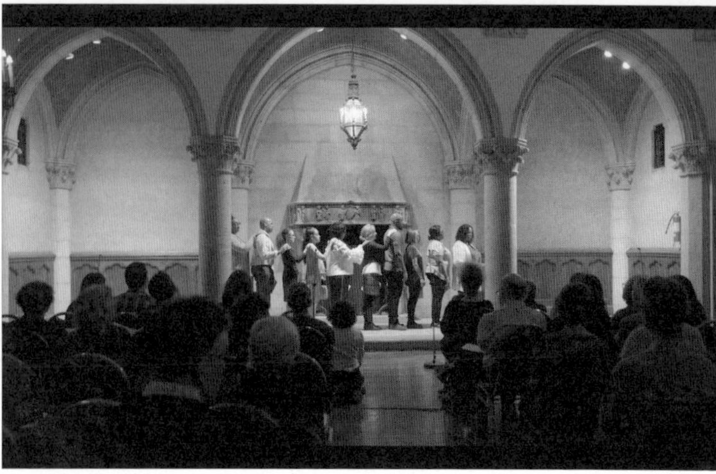

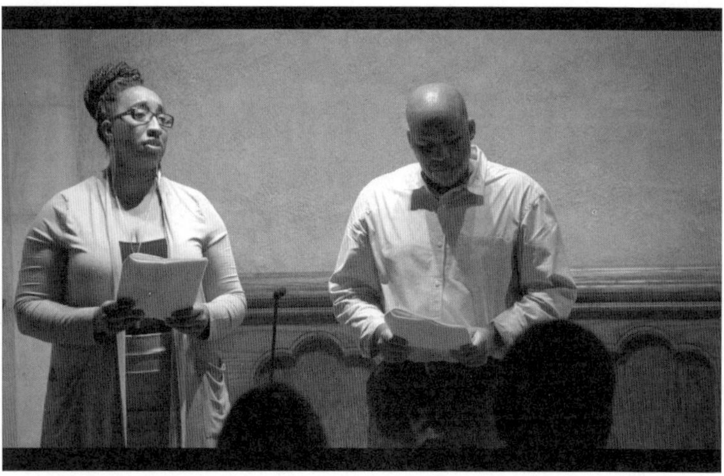

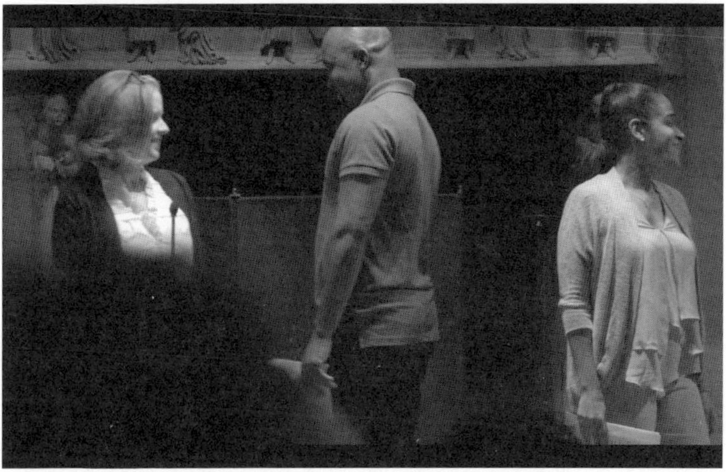

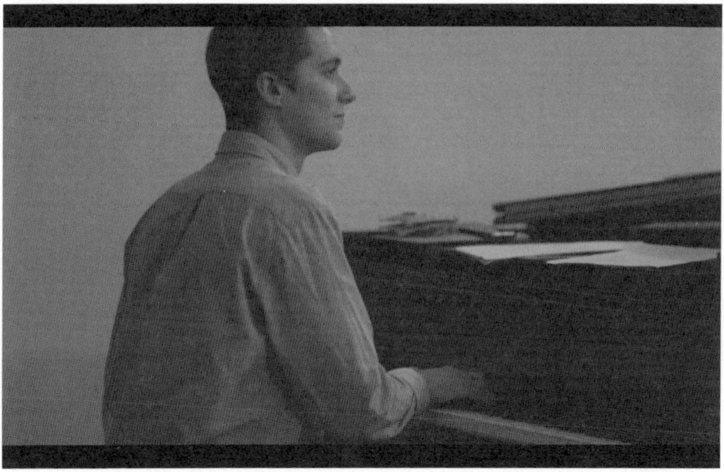

9. THIS IS THE TIME

SONG 4

Performers return to the line

Keresha
I'm going to take this time.

Everyone goes down the line, repeating
"I'm going to take this time."

Everyone rests their head on the person to their left (Agnes + Melody rest their heads on each other)

After Melody goes, everyone takes ten breaths together

A bow

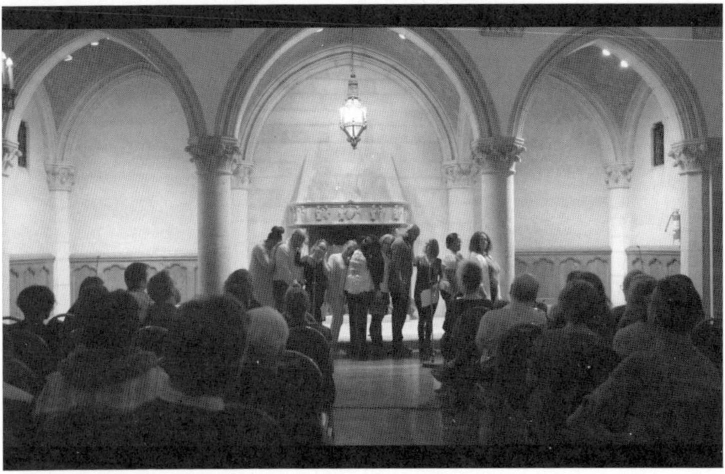

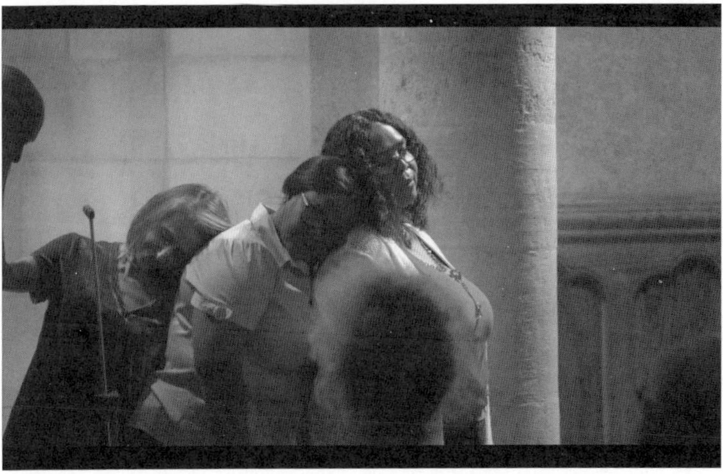

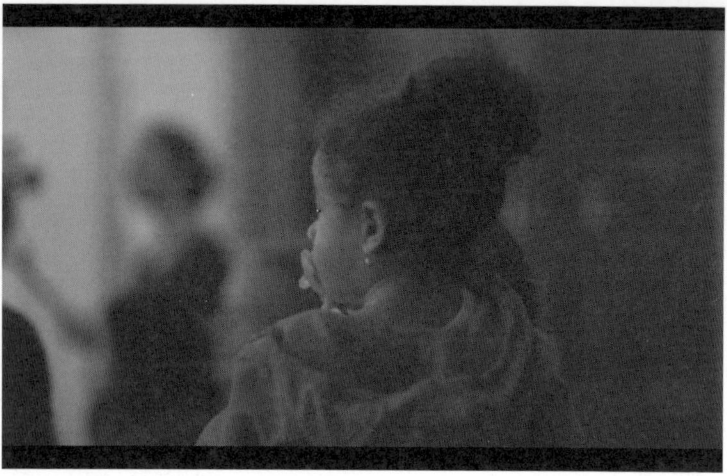

Performance stills and script, *A Knock on the Door*
Riverside Church, New York City

When I was in Maine for the wedding, I rented a room from a woman who lived alone. She had a bowlcut and an outdoor bathtub. When I arrived, she insisted on giving me a tour of the town. As we drove past the one-room library she said, *I really should read more novels. For the sake of my friendships.*

I loved this way of thinking about cultural knowledge. Of personal growth. That my insights become your insights.

I believe this. That we grow for the sake of something bigger than us.

I forgot to tell Hope that our childhood piano teacher died. For some reason, even after all this, I can't bring myself to tell her.

On Process and Responsibility

Stages brings together the words and ideas of many real people. Behind the scenes of this text and Thick Press are questions about care. How can we care for people at the end of their lives? How can we care for our careworkers? How can we bring care to the forefront of political and civic life? And then, in making a book, how can we adopt a stance of caring responsibility to everyone involved?

In partnership with the Hebrew Home, we asked everyone interviewed for permission to include their words and photographic image for publication. Everybody reviewed their interview, removed or changed anything they chose, and decided whether they wanted to attribute their name to their words or remain anonymous.

Staff members often chose to remove brief passages that expressed negative feelings. We did not pressure them to keep those passages. Although we miss the richness of those sections, we believe books are as strong as their process. This feels especially important given that the purpose of Rachel's original performance project was to foster trust and resilience among staff at the nursing home.

Rachel's personal writings are driven by a different impulse, but our guiding questions remain. We shared the manuscript with anyone described in the book, and spoke with everyone about their inclusion and portrayal to ensure their comfort. In some instances, especially when we could not speak together, we altered names and identifying descriptions in order to preserve privacy.

We asked family members to make decisions on behalf of the dead. We sought the blessing of the dead.

Finally, we invited several trusted friends and colleagues to offer feedback on the ethics of our methodology.

We did all this while acknowledging the imperfection of these approaches.

Thank you to everyone who helped us!

—Rachel & Thick Press

Images & Acknowledgments

Thank you Maria for bringing me to the nursing home. Thank you Barbara and Kate and all our seniors for making *The Birds* with me. Thank you Mary, Catherine, and Joy at the Hebrew Home for creating room for work, art and healing to intertwine.

I fell into the best hands with Thick Press. Thank you Erin and Julie for making a place in the world for books like this to belong. Thank you Erin, for seeing *Stages* as a book and considering every word with astonishing attention. I've learned so much from you about editing and correspondence as art and care work.

Thank you to my parents, Helen and Barry, for providing security for me to work for the poor-paying causes I believe in. Thank you Rachel and Emily for being my collaborators and teachers. Thank you Coleman for making spiritual music. Thank you Ike for your kindness. Thank you Claire for the quiet house. Thank you to the Blue Mountain Center. Thank you Cassie, Sarah, Laurelin and always, Zoe, for reading.

A Knock on the Door was created by Rachel Kauder Nalebuff in collaboration with the staff of the Hebrew Home at Riverdale. It was commissioned by the Hebrew Home at Riverdale in partnership with Reimagine End of Life 2018. Music by Coleman Zurkowski. Movement by Rachel Bernsen.

This publication was made possible, in part, by a faculty grant from Otis College of Art and Design and a contribution from Cassandra and Carl Segal.

Special thanks from Thick Press to Jenny Jackson and Deb Rubenstein.

About the Author

Rachel Kauder Nalebuff is a writer working often in the realms of performance and oral history. She is the editor of *My Little Red Book* (Hachette, 2009), a collection of people's first period stories, and co-editor of *The Feminist Utopia Project* (Feminist Press, 2015) with Alexandra Brodsky. She runs a memoir program for seniors with Caitlin Ryan O'Connell and many friends through the New York City Department of Aging.

About the Press

Thick Press publishes unusual books about care work and the work of care. We are Erin Segal, a social worker, and Julie Cho, a graphic designer.